Defoe Abbott Marx Hardy Machiavelli Montaigne Chesterton Cooper Emerson Joyce Austen Hugo Eliot Grimm Melville Haggard Molière

Stoker Carroll Christie Maupassant Byron Schiller Wilde Engels Smith Kafka

Garnett Fitzgerald Hawthorne Hall Goethe Einstein Dostoyevsky Willis Cotton Kipling Doyle

Baum Henry Nietzsche Balzac Leslie Dumas Flaubert Turgenev Crane Stockton Vatsyayana Verne Burroughs Whitman Gogol Vinci Curtis Tocqueville Busch Homer Widger Tolstoy Darwin Thoreau Twain Potter Freud Zola Lawrence Plato Scott Harte Kant Jowett Stevenson Dickens Hesse Burton Andersen Descartes Cervantes London Voltaire Cooke Poe Aristotle Wells Hale James Hastings Bunner Shakespeare Irving Richter Chambers da Dante Chekhov Swift Shaw Wodehouse Benedict Alcott Doré Pushkin Newton

 tredition®

tredition was established in 2006 by Sandra Latusseck and Soenke Schulz. Based in Hamburg, Germany, tredition offers publishing solutions to authors and publishing houses, combined with world-wide distribution of printed and digital book content. tredition is uniquely positioned to enable authors and publishing houses to create books on their own terms and without conventional manu-facturing risks.

For more information please visit: www.tredition.com

TREDITION CLASSICS

This book is part of the TREDITION CLASSICS series. The creators of this series are united by passion for literature and driven by the intention of making all public domain books available in printed format again - worldwide. Most TREDITION CLASSICS titles have been out of print and off the bookstore shelves for decades. At tredi-tion we believe that a great book never goes out of style and that its value is eternal. Several mostly non-profit literature projects pro-vide content to tredition. To support their good work, tredition donates a portion of the proceeds from each sold copy. As a reader of a TREDITION CLASSICS book, you support our mission to save many of the amazing works of world literature from oblivion. See all available books at www.tredition.com.

Project Gutenberg

The content for this book has been graciously provided by Project Gutenberg. Project Gutenberg is a non-profit organization founded by Michael Hart in 1971 at the University of Illinois. The mission of Project Gutenberg is simple: To encourage the creation and distribu-tion of eBooks. Project Gutenberg is the first and largest collection of public domain eBooks.

In Our First Year of the War Messages and Addresses to the Congress and the People, March 5, 1917 to January 6, 1918

Woodrow Wilson

Imprint

This book is part of TREDITION CLASSICS

Author: Woodrow Wilson
Cover design: Buchgut, Berlin – Germany

Publisher: tredition GmbH, Hamburg - Germany
ISBN: 978-3-8472-1718-3

www.tredition.com
www.tredition.de

IN OUR
FIRST YEAR OF WAR

MESSAGES AND ADDRESSES TO
THE CONGRESS AND THE PEOPLE
MARCH 5, 1917, TO JANUARY 8, 1918

BY

WOODROW WILSON

PRESIDENT OF THE UNITED STATES

Frontispiece from drawing by
WILFRID MUIR EVANS

HARPER & BROTHERS PUBLISHERS
NEW YORK AND LONDON

CONTENTS

FOREWORD

This book opens with the second inaugural address and contains the President's messages and addresses since the United States was forced to take up arms against Germany. These pages may be said to picture not only official phases of the great crisis, but also the highest significance of liberty and democracy and the reactions of President and people to the great developments of the times. The second Inaugural Address with its sense of solemn responsibility serves as a prophecy as well as prelude to the declaration of war and the message to the people which followed so soon.

The extracts from the Conscription Proclamation, the messages on Conservation and the Fixing of Prices, the Appeal to Business Interests, the Address to the Federation of Labor and the Railroad messages present the solid every-day realities and the vast responsibilities of war-time as they affect every American. These are concrete messages which should be at hand for frequent reference, just as the uplift and inspiration of lofty appeals like the Memorial Day and Flag Day addresses should be a constant source of inspiration. There are also the clarifying and vigorous definitions of American purpose afforded in utterances like the statement to Russia, the reply to the communication of the Pope, and, most emphatically, the President's restatement of War Aims on January 8th. These and other state papers from the early spring of 1917 to January, 1918, have a significance and value in this collected form which has been attested by the many requests that have come to Harper & Brothers, as President Wilson's publishers, for a war volume of the President's messages to follow *Why We Are At War*.

As a matter of course, the President has been consulted in regard to the plan of publication, and the conditions which he requested have been observed. For title, arrangement, headings, and like details the publishers are responsible. They have held the publication of the President's words of enlightenment and inspiration to be a public service. And they think that there is no impropriety in adding that in the case of this book, and *Why We Are At War*, the American Red Cross receives all author's royalties.

In the case of the former book the evolution of events which led to war was illustrated in messages from January to April 15th. In the preparation of this book, which begins with the second inaugural, it has seemed desirable to present practically all the messages of war-time, and therefore three papers are included which appeared in the former and smaller book, in addition to the twenty-one messages and addresses which have been collected for this volume.

IN OUR FIRST YEAR
OF WAR

IN OUR FIRST YEAR
OF WAR

I

THE SECOND INAUGURAL ADDRESS

(March 5, 1917)

My Fellow-citizens,--The four years which have elapsed since last I stood in this place have been crowded with counsel and action of the most vital interest and consequence. Perhaps no equal period in our history has been so fruitful of important reforms in our economic and industrial life or so full of significant changes in the spirit and purpose of our political action. We have sought very thoughtfully to set our house in order, correct the grosser errors and abuses of our industrial life, liberate and quicken the processes of our national genius and energy, and lift our politics to a broader view of the people's essential interests. It is a record of singular variety and 2singular distinction. But I shall not attempt to review it. It speaks for itself and will be of increasing influence as the years go by. This is not the time for retrospect. It is time, rather, to speak our thoughts and purposes concerning the present and the immediate future.

A COSMOPOLITAN EPOCH AT HAND

Although we have centered counsel and action with such unusual concentration and success upon the great problems of domestic legislation to which we addressed ourselves four years ago, other matters have more and more forced themselves upon our attention, matters lying outside our own life as a nation and over which we had no control, but which, despite our wish to keep free of them, have drawn us more and more irresistibly into their own current and influence.

It has been impossible to avoid them. They have affected the life of the whole world. They have shaken men everywhere with a passion and an apprehension they never knew before. It has been hard to preserve calm counsel while the thought of our own people swayed this way and that under their influence. We are a composite and cosmopolitan people. We are of the blood of all the nations that are at war. The currents of our thoughts as well as the currents of our trade run quick at 3all seasons back and forth between us and them. The war inevitably set its mark from the first alike upon our minds, our industries, our commerce, our politics, and our social action. To be indifferent to it or independent of it was out of the question.

And yet all the while we have been conscious that we were not part of it. In that consciousness, despite many divisions, we have drawn closer together. We have been deeply wronged upon the seas, but we have not wished to wrong or injure in return; have retained throughout the consciousness of standing in some sort apart, intent upon an interest that transcended the immediate issues of the war itself. As some of the injuries done us have become intolerable, we have still been clear that we wished nothing for ourselves that we were not ready to demand for all mankind,--fair dealing, justice, the freedom to live and be at ease against organized wrong.

It is in this spirit and with this thought that we have grown more and more aware, more and more certain that the part we wished to play was the part of those who mean to vindicate and fortify peace. We have been obliged to arm ourselves to make good our claim to a certain minimum of right and of freedom of action. We stand firm in armed neutrality since it seems that in no other way we can demonstrate what it is we insist upon 4and cannot forego. We may even be drawn on, by circumstances, not by our own purpose or desire, to a more active assertion of our rights as we see them and a more immediate association with the great struggle itself. But nothing will alter our thought or our purpose. They are too clear to be obscured. They are too deeply rooted in the principles of our national life to be altered. We desire neither conquest nor advantage. We wish nothing that can be had only at the cost of another people. We have always professed unselfish purpose and we covet the opportunity to prove that our professions are sincere.

THE SPIRIT OF CO-OPERATION

There are many things still to do at home, to clarify our own politics and give new vitality to the industrial processes of our own life, and we shall do them as time and opportunity serve; but we realize that the greatest things that remain to be done must be done with the whole world for stage and in co-operation with the wide and universal forces of mankind, and we are making our spirits ready for those things. They will follow in the immediate wake of the war itself and will set civilization up again. We are provincials no longer. The tragical events of the thirty months of vital turmoil through which we have just passed have made us citizens of the 5world. There can be no turning back. Our own fortunes as a nation are involved, whether we would have it so or not.

And yet we are not the less Americans on that account. We shall be the more American if we but remain true to the principles in which we have been bred. They are not the principles of a province or of a single continent. We have known and boasted all along that they were the principles of a liberated mankind. These, therefore, are the things we shall stand for, whether in war or in peace:

OUR NATIONAL PLATFORM

That all nations are equally interested in the peace of the world and in the political stability of free peoples, and equally responsible for their maintenance;

That the essential principle of peace is the actual equality of nations in all matters of right or privilege;

That peace cannot securely or justly rest upon an armed balance of power;

That Governments derive all their just powers from the consent of the governed and that no other powers should be supported by the common thought, purpose or power of the family of nations;

That the seas should be equally free and safe for the use of all peoples, under rules set up by common agreement and consent, and 6that, so far as practicable, they should be accessible to all upon equal terms;

That national armaments should be limited to the necessities of national order and domestic safety;

That the community of interest and of power upon which peace must henceforth depend imposes upon each nation the duty of seeing to it that all influences proceeding from its own citizens meant to encourage or assist revolution in other states should be sternly and effectually suppressed and prevented.

A UNITY OF PURPOSE AND ACTION

I need not argue these principles to you, my fellow-countrymen: they are your own, part and parcel of your own thinking and your own motive in affairs. They spring up native amongst us. Upon this as a platform of purpose and of action we can stand together.

And it is imperative that we should stand together. We are being forged into a new unity amidst the fires that now blaze throughout the world. In their ardent heat we shall, in God's providence, let us hope, be purged of faction and division, purified of the errant humors of party and of private interest, and shall stand forth in the days to come with a new dignity of national pride and spirit. Let each man see to it that the dedication is in his own heart, the high purpose of the nation 7in his own mind, ruler of his own will and desire.

I stand here and have taken the high and solemn oath to which you have been audience because the people of the United States have chosen me for this august delegation of power and have by their gracious judgment named me their leader in affairs. I know now what the task means. I realize to the full the responsibility which it involves. I pray God I may be given the wisdom and the prudence to do my duty in the true spirit of this great people. I am their servant and can succeed only as they sustain and guide me by their confidence and their counsel. The thing I shall count upon, the thing without which neither counsel nor action will avail, is the unity of America--an America united in feeling, in purpose, and in its vision of duty, of opportunity, and of service. We are to beware of all men who would turn the tasks and the necessities of the nation to their own private profit or use them for the building up of private power; beware that no faction or disloyal intrigue break the harmony or embarrass the spirit of our people; beware that our Government be kept pure and incorrupt in all its parts. United alike in the conception of our duty and in the high resolve to perform it in the face of all men, let us dedicate ourselves to the great task to which we must now set our 8hand. For myself I beg your tolerance, your countenance, and your united aid. The shadows that now lie dark upon our path will soon be dispelled and we shall walk with the light all about us if we be but true to ourselves--to ourselves as we have wished to be known in the counsels of the world and in the thought of all those who love liberty and justice and the right exalted.

9

II

WE MUST ACCEPT WAR

(Message to the Congress, April 2, 1917)

Gentlemen of the Congress,--I have called the Congress into extraordinary session because there are serious, very serious, choices of policy to be made, and made immediately, which it was neither right nor constitutionally permissible that I should assume the responsibility of making.

On the 3d of February last I officially laid before you the extraordinary announcement of the Imperial German Government that on and after the first day of February it was its purpose to put aside all restraints of law or of humanity and use its submarines to sink every vessel that sought to approach either the ports of Great Britain and Ireland or the western coasts of Europe or any of the ports controlled by the enemies of Germany within the Mediterranean. That had seemed to be the object of the German submarine warfare earlier in the war, but since April of last year the Imperial Government had somewhat restrained the 10commanders of its undersea craft in conformity with its promise then given to us that passenger-boats should not be sunk, and that due warning would be given to all other vessels which its submarines might seek to destroy when no resistance was offered or escape attempted, and care taken that their crews were given at least a fair chance to save their lives in their open boats.

The precautions taken were meager and haphazard enough, as was proved in distressing instance after instance in the progress of the cruel and unmanly business, but a certain degree of restraint was observed.

GERMANY'S RUTHLESS POLICY

The new policy has swept every restriction aside. Vessels of every kind, whatever their flag, their character, their cargo, their destination, their errand, have been ruthlessly sent to the bottom without warning, and without thought of help or mercy for those on board, the vessels of friendly neutrals along with those of belligerents. Even hospital-ships and ships carrying relief to the sorely bereaved and stricken people of Belgium, though the latter were provided with safe conduct through the proscribed areas by the German Government itself and were distinguished by unmistakable marks of identity, have been sunk with the same reckless lack of compassion or of principle.

11

I was for a little while unable to believe that such things would, in fact, be done by any Government that had hitherto subscribed to the humane practices of civilized nations. International law had its origin in the attempt to set up some law which would be respected and observed upon the seas, where no nation had right of dominion, and where lay the free highways of the world. By painful stage after stage has that law been built up with meager enough results, indeed, after all was accomplished that could be accomplished, but always with a clear view at least of what the heart and conscience of mankind demanded.

This minimum of right the German Government has swept aside under the plea of retaliation and necessity, and because it had no weapons which it could use at sea except these, which it is impossible to employ as it is employing them without throwing to the winds all scruples of humanity or of respect for the understandings that were supposed to underlie the intercourse of the world.

I am not now thinking of the loss of property involved, immense and serious as that is, but only of the wanton and wholesale destruction of the lives of non-combatants, men, women and children engaged in pursuits which have always, even in the darkest periods of modern history, been deemed innocent and legitimate.

12

Property can be paid for; the lives of peaceful and innocent people cannot be.

GERMAN WARFARE AGAINST MANKIND

The present German warfare against commerce is a warfare against mankind. It is a war against all nations. American ships have been sunk, American lives taken, in ways which it has stirred us very deeply to learn of, but the ships and people of other neutral and friendly nations have been sunk and overwhelmed in the waters in the same way. There has been no discrimination. The challenge is to all mankind. Each nation must decide for itself how it will meet it. The choice we make for ourselves must be made with a moderation of counsel and a temperateness of judgment befitting our character and our motives as a nation. We must put excited feeling away.

Our motive will not be revenge or the victorious assertion of the physical might of the nation, but only the vindication of right, of human right, of which we are only a single champion.

When I addressed the Congress on the 26th of February last I thought that it would suffice to assert our neutral rights with arms, our right to use the seas against unlawful interference, our right to keep our people safe against unlawful violence. But armed neutrality, 13 it now appears, is impracticable. Because submarines are in effect outlaws when used as the German submarines have been used against merchant shipping, it is impossible to defend ships against their attacks as the law of nations has assumed that merchantmen would defend themselves against privateers or cruisers, visible craft giving chase upon the open sea.

It is common prudence in such circumstances, grim necessity, indeed, to endeavor to destroy them before they have shown their own intention. They must be dealt with upon sight, if dealt with at all.

The German Government denies the right of neutrals to use arms at all within the areas of the sea which it has proscribed, even in the defense of rights which no modern publicist has ever before questioned their right to defend. The intimation is conveyed that the armed guards which we have placed on our merchant-ships will be treated as beyond the pale of law and subject to be dealt with as pirates would be.

Armed neutrality is ineffectual enough at best; in such circumstances and in the face of such pretensions it is worse than ineffectual; it is likely to produce what it was meant to prevent; it is practically certain to draw us into the war without either the rights or the effectiveness of belligerents.

14

There is one choice we cannot make, we are incapable of making: we will not choose the path of submission and suffer the most sacred rights of our nation and our people to be ignored or violated. The wrongs against which we now array ourselves are not common wrongs; they reach out to the very roots of human life.

BELLIGERENCY THRUST UPON US

With a profound sense of the solemn and even tragical character of the step I am taking and of the grave responsibilities which it involves, but in unhesitating obedience to what I deem my constitutional duty, I advise that the Congress declare the recent course of the Imperial German Government to be in fact nothing less than war against the Government and people of the United States. That it formally accept the status of belligerent which has thus been thrust upon it and that it take immediate steps not only to put the country in a more thorough state of defense, but also to exert all its power and employ all its resources to bring the Government of the German Empire to terms and end the war.

WHAT THIS WILL INVOLVE

What this will involve is clear. It will involve the utmost practicable co-operation in counsel and action with the Governments now 15at war with Germany, and as incident to that the extension to those Governments of the most liberal financial credits in order that our resources may so far as possible be added to theirs.

It will involve the organization and mobilization of all the material resources of the country to supply the materials of war and serve the incidental needs of the nation in the most abundant and yet the most economical and efficient way possible.

It will involve the immediate full equipment of the navy in all respects, but particularly in supplying it with the best means of dealing with the enemy's submarines.

It will involve the immediate addition to the armed forces of the United States already provided for by law in case of war at least 500,000 men, who should, in my opinion, be chosen upon the principle of universal liability to service, and also the authorization of subsequent additional increments of equal force so soon as they may be needed and can be handled in training.

It will involve also, of course, the granting of adequate credits to the Government, sustained, I hope, so far as they can equitably be sustained by the present generation, by well-conceived taxation. I say sustained so far as may be equitable by taxation because it seems to me that it would be most unwise to base 16the credits which will now be necessary entirely on money borrowed.

It is our duty, I most respectfully urge, to protect our people so far as we may against the very serious hardships and evils which would be likely to arise out of the inflation which would be produced by vast loans.

In carrying out the measures by which these things are to be accomplished we should keep constantly in mind the wisdom of interfering as little as possible in our own preparation and in the equipment of our own military forces with the duty--for it will be a very practical duty--of supplying the nations already at war with Germany with the materials which they can obtain only from us or by our assistance. They are in the field and we should help them in every way to be effective there.

I shall take the liberty of suggesting, through the several executive departments of the Government, for the consideration of your committees measures for the accomplishment of the several objects I have mentioned. I hope that it will be your pleasure to deal with them as having been framed after very careful thought by the branch of the Government upon which the responsibility of conducting the war and safeguarding the nation will most directly fall.

17

OUR MOTIVES AND OBJECTS

While we do these things, these deeply momentous things, let us be very clear and make very clear to all the world what our motives and our objects are. My own thought has not been driven from its habitual and normal course by the unhappy events of the last two months, and I do not believe that the thought of the nation has been altered or clouded by them.

I have exactly the same thing in mind now that I had in mind when I addressed the Senate on the 22d of January last; the same that I had in mind when I addressed the Congress on the 3d of February and on the 26th of February.

Our object now, as then, is to vindicate the principles of peace and justice in the life of the world as against selfish and autocratic power and to set up amongst the really free and self-governed peoples of the world such a concert of purpose and of action as will henceforth insure the observance of those principles.

Neutrality is no longer feasible or desirable where the peace of the world is involved and the freedom of its peoples, and the menace to that peace and freedom lies in the existence of autocratic Governments backed by organized force which is controlled wholly by their will, not by the will of their people. We have 18seen the last of neutrality in such circumstances.

We are at the beginning of an age in which it will be insisted that the same standards of conduct and of responsibility for wrong done shall be observed among nations and their Governments that are observed among the individual citizens of civilized states.

We have no quarrel with the German people. We have no feeling toward them but one of sympathy and friendship. It was not upon their impulse that their Government acted in entering this war. It was not with their previous knowledge or approval.

It was a war determined upon as wars used to be determined upon in the old, unhappy days when peoples were nowhere consulted by their rulers and wars were provoked and waged in the interest of dynasties or of little groups of ambitious men who were accustomed to use their fellow-men as pawns and tools.

Self-governed nations do not fill their neighbor states with spies or set the course of intrigue to bring about some critical posture of affairs which will give them an opportunity to strike and make conquest. Such designs can be successfully worked only under cover and where no one has the right to ask questions.

Cunningly contrived plans of deception or 19aggression, carried, it may be, from generation to generation, can be worked out and kept from the light only within the privacy of courts or behind the carefully guarded confidences of a narrow and privileged class. They are happily impossible where public opinion commands and insists upon full information concerning all the nation's affairs.

PEACE THROUGH FREE PEOPLES

A steadfast concert for peace can never be maintained except by a partnership of democratic nations. No autocratic Government could be trusted to keep faith within it or observe its covenants. It must be a league of honor, a partnership of opinion. Intrigue would eat its vitals away, the plottings of inner circles who could plan what they would and render account to no one would be a corruption seated at its very heart. Only free peoples can hold their purpose and their honor steady to a common end and prefer the interests of mankind to any narrow interest of their own.

Does not every American feel that assurance has been added to our hope for the future peace of the world by the wonderful and heartening things that have been happening within the last few weeks in Russia?

Russia was known by those who know it best to have been always in fact democratic at heart, in all the vital habits of her thought, 20in all the intimate relationships of her people that spoke their natural instinct, their habitual attitude toward life.

Autocracy that crowned the summit of her political structure, long as it had stood and terrible as was the reality of its power, was not in fact Russian in origin, in character or purpose; and now it has been shaken and the great, generous Russian people have been added, in all their native majesty and might, to the forces that are fighting for freedom in the world, for justice and for peace. Here is a fit partner for a league of honor.

One of the things that have served to convince us that the Prussian autocracy was not and could never be our friend is that from the very outset of the present war it has filled our unsuspecting communities and even our offices of Government with spies and set criminal intrigues everywhere afoot against our national unity of council, our peace within and without, our industries and our commerce.

Indeed, it is now evident that its spies were here even before the war began, and it is, unhappily, not a matter of conjecture, but a fact proved in our courts of justice, that the intrigues which have more than once come perilously near to disturbing the peace and dislocating the industries of the country have been carried on at the instigation, with the support, and even under the personal direction, of official 21agents of the Imperial German Government accredited to the Government of the United States.

Even in checking these things and trying to extirpate them we have sought to put the most generous interpretation possible upon them because we knew that their source lay, not in any hostile feeling or purpose of the German people toward us (who were, no doubt, as ignorant of them as we ourselves were), but only in the selfish designs of a Government that did what it pleased and told its people nothing. But they have played their part in serving to convince us at last that that Government entertains no real friendship for us and means to act against our peace and security at its convenience. That it means to stir up enemies against us at our very doors the intercepted note to the German Minister at Mexico City is eloquent evidence.

A CHALLENGE OF HOSTILE PURPOSE

We are accepting this challenge of hostile purpose because we know that in such a Government, following such methods, we can never have a friend; and that in the presence of its organized power, always lying in wait to accomplish we know not what purpose, there can be no assured security for the democratic Governments of the world.

We are now about to accept the gage of 22battle with this natural foe to liberty, and shall, if necessary, spend the whole force of the nation to check and nullify its pretensions and its power. We are glad, now that we see the facts with no veil of false pretense about them, to fight thus for the ultimate peace of the world and for the liberation of its peoples, the German people included; for the rights of nations great and small and the privilege of men everywhere to choose their way of life and of obedience. The world must be made safe for democracy. Its peace must be planted upon the trusted foundations of political liberty.

We have no selfish ends to serve. We desire no conquest, no dominion. We seek no indemnities for ourselves, no material compensation for the sacrifices we shall freely make. We are but one of the champions of the rights of mankind. We shall be satisfied when those rights have been made as secure as the faith and the freedom of the nation can make them.

Just because we fight without rancor and without selfish objects, seeking nothing for ourselves but what we shall wish to share with all free peoples, we shall, I feel confident, conduct our operations as belligerents without passion and ourselves observe with proud punctilio the principles of right and of fair play we profess to be fighting for.

I have said nothing of the Governments allied with the Imperial Government of Germany because they have not made war upon us or challenged us to defend our right and our honor.

The Austro-Hungarian Government has indeed avowed its unqualified indorsement and acceptance of the reckless and lawless submarine warfare adopted now without disguise by the Imperial German Government, and it has therefore not been possible for this Government to receive Count Tarnowski, the ambassador recently accredited to this Government by the Imperial and Royal Government of Austria-Hungary; but that Government has not actually engaged in warfare against citizens of the United States on the seas, and I take the liberty, for the present at least, of postponing a discussion of our relations with the authorities at Vienna.

OPPOSITION TO THE GERMAN GOVERNMENT

FRIENDSHIP TOWARD THE GERMAN PEOPLE

We enter this war only where we are clearly forced into it because there are no other means of defending our rights.

It will be all the easier for us to conduct ourselves as belligerents in a high spirit of right and fairness because we act without animus, not in enmity toward a people or with the desire to bring any injury or disadvantage 24upon them, but only in armed opposition to an irresponsible Government which has thrown aside all considerations of humanity and of right and is running amuck.

We are, let me say again, the sincere friends of the German people, and shall desire nothing so much as the early re-establishment of intimate relations of mutual advantage between us--however hard it may be for them, for the time being, to believe that this is spoken from our hearts. We have borne with their present Government through all these bitter months because of that friendship--exercising a patience and forbearance which would otherwise have been impossible.

We shall, happily, still have an opportunity to prove that friendship in our daily attitude and actions toward the millions of men and women of German birth and native sympathy who live amongst us and share our life, and we shall be proud to prove it toward all who are, in fact, loyal to their neighbors and to the Government in the hour of test. They are, most of them, as true and loyal Americans as if they had never known any other fealty or allegiance. They will be prompt to stand with us in rebuking and restraining the few who may be of a different mind and purpose. If there should be disloyalty it will be dealt with with a firm hand of stern repression; but, if it lifts its head at all, it will lift it only here 25and there and without countenance except from a lawless and malignant few.

RIGHT MORE PRECIOUS THAN PEACE

It is a distressing and oppressive duty, gentlemen of the Congress, which I have performed in thus addressing you. There are, it may be, many months of fiery trial and sacrifice ahead of us. It is a fearful thing to lead this great, peaceful people into war, into the most terrible and disastrous of all wars, civilization itself seeming to be in the balance. But the right is more precious than peace, and we shall fight for the things which we have always carried nearest our hearts--for democracy, for the right of those who submit to authority to have a voice in their own governments, for the rights and liberties of small nations, for a universal dominion of right by such a concert of free peoples as shall bring peace and safety to all nations and make the world itself at last free.

To such a task we can dedicate our lives and our fortunes, everything that we are and everything that we have, with the pride of those who know that the day has come when America is privileged to spend her blood and her might for the principles that gave her birth and happiness and the peace which she has treasured. God helping her, she can do no other.

26

III

A STATE OF WAR

(The President's Proclamation of April 6, 1917)

Whereas, the Congress of the United States, in the exercise of the constitutional authority vested in them, have resolved by joint resolution of the Senate and House of Representatives, bearing date this day, that a state of war between the United States and the Imperial German Government, which has been thrust upon the United States, is hereby formally declared;

Whereas, It is provided by Section 4067 of the Revised Statutes as follows:

> Whenever there is declared a war between the United States and any foreign nation or Government, or any invasion or predatory incursion is perpetrated, attempted or threatened against the territory of the United States by any foreign nation or Government, and the President makes public proclamation of the event, all natives, citizens, denizens or subjects of a hostile nation or Government being male of the age of fourteen years and upward who shall be within the United States and not actually naturalized shall be liable to be apprehended, restrained secured and removed as alien enemies.

27

The President is authorized in any such event, by his proclamation thereof or other public acts, to direct the conduct to be observed on the part of the United States toward the aliens who become so liable; the manner and degree of the restraint to which they shall be subject and in what cases and upon what security their residence shall be permitted and to provide for the removal of those who, not being permitted to reside within the United States, refuse or neglect to depart therefrom, and to establish any such regulations which are found necessary in the premises and for the public safety;

Whereas, By Sections 4068, 4069, and 4070 of the Revised Statutes further provision is made relative to alien enemies;

Now, therefore, I, Woodrow Wilson, President of the United States of America, do hereby proclaim to all whom it may concern that a state of war exists between the United States and the Imperial German Government, and I do specially direct all officers, civil or military, of the United States that they exercise vigilance and zeal in the discharge of the duties incident to such a state of war, and I do, moreover, earnestly appeal to all American citizens that they, in loyal devotion to their country, dedicated from its foundation to the principles of liberty and justice, uphold the laws of the land and give undivided and willing 28support to those measures which may be adopted by the constitutional authorities in prosecuting the war to a successful issue and in obtaining a secure and just peace;

And acting under and by virtue of the authority vested in me by the Constitution of the United States and the said sections of the Revised Statutes:

I do hereby further proclaim and direct that the conduct to be observed on the part of the United States toward all natives, citizens, denizens or subjects of Germany, being male, of the age of fourteen years and upward, who shall be within the United States and not actually naturalized, who for the purpose of this proclamation and under such sections of the Revised Statutes are termed alien enemies, shall be as follows:

> All alien enemies are enjoined to preserve the peace toward the United States and to refrain from crime against the public safety and from violating the laws of the United States and of the States and Territories thereof, and to refrain from actual hostility or giving information, aid or comfort to the enemies of the United States, and to comply strictly with the regulations which are hereby or which may be from time to time promulgated by the President, and so long as they shall conduct them-

selves in accordance with law they shall be undisturbed in the peaceful pursuit of their lives and occupations and be accorded the consideration due to all peaceful and law-abiding persons, except so far as restrictions may be necessary for their own protection and for the safety of the United States, and toward such alien 29enemies as conduct themselves in accordance with law all citizens of the United States are enjoined to preserve the peace and to treat them with all such friendliness as may be compatible with loyalty and allegiance to the United States.

And all alien enemies who fail to conduct themselves as so enjoined, in addition to all other penalties prescribed by law, shall be liable to restraint or to give security or to remove and depart from the United States in the manner prescribed by Sections 4069 and 4070 of the Revised Statutes and as prescribed in the regulations duly promulgated by the President.

And, pursuant to the authority vested in me, I hereby declare and establish the following regulations, which I find necessary in the premises and for the public safety:

First. An alien enemy shall not have in his possession at any time or place any firearms, weapons or implement of war, or component parts thereof; ammunition, Maxim or other silencer, arms or explosives or material used in the manufacture of explosives.

Second. An alien enemy shall not have in his possession at any time or place, or use or operate, any aircraft or wireless apparatus, or any form of signaling device, or any form of cipher code or any paper, document or book written or printed in cipher, or in which there may be invisible writing.

Third. All property found in the possession of an alien enemy in violation of the foregoing regulations shall be subject to seizure by the United States.

Fourth. An alien enemy shall not approach or be found within one-half of a mile of any Federal or State fort, camp, arsenal, aircraft station, Government or naval vessel, navy-yard, factory or workshop for the 30manufacture of munitions of war or of any products for the use of the army or navy.

Fifth. An alien enemy shall not write, print or publish any attack or threat against the Government or Congress of the United States, or either branch thereof, or against the measures or policy of the United States, or against the persons or property of any person in the military, naval or civil service of the United States, or of the States or Territories, or of the District of Columbia, or of the municipal governments therein.

Sixth. An alien enemy shall not commit or abet any hostile acts against the United States, or give information, aid or comfort to its enemies.

Seventh. An alien enemy shall not reside in or continue to reside in, to remain in or enter any locality which the President may from time to time designate by an executive order as a prohibitive area in which residence by an alien enemy shall be found by him to constitute a danger to the public peace and safety of the United States except by permit from the President and except under such limitations or restrictions as the President may prescribe.

Eighth. An alien enemy whom the President shall have reasonable cause to believe to be aiding or about to aid the enemy, or to be at large to the danger of the public peace or safety of the United States, or to have violated or to be about to violate any of these regulations, shall remove to any location designated by the President by executive order, and shall not remove therefrom without permit, or shall depart from the United States if so required by the President.

Ninth. No alien enemy shall depart from the United States until he shall have received such permit as the President shall prescribe, or except under order of a Court, Judge or Justice, under Sections 4069 and 4070 of the Revised Statutes.

Tenth. No alien enemy shall land in or enter the 31United States except under such restrictions and at such places as the President may prescribe.

Eleventh. If necessary to prevent violation of the regulations, all alien enemies will be obliged to register.

Twelfth. An alien enemy whom there may be reasonable cause to believe to be aiding or about to aid the enemy, or to be at large to the danger of the public peace or safety, or who violates or who attempts to violate or of whom there is reasonable grounds to believe that he is about to violate any regulation to be promulgated by the President or any criminal law of the United States or of the States or Territories thereof, will be subject to summary arrest by the United States, by the United States Marshal or his deputy or such other officers as the President shall designate, and to confinement in such penitentiary, prison, jail, military camp, or other place of detention as may be directed by the President.

This proclamation and the regulations herein contained shall extend and apply to all land and water, continental or insular, in any way within the jurisdiction of the United States.

32

36

IV

"SPEAK, ACT AND SERVE TOGETHER"

(*Message to the American People, April 15, 1917*)

My Fellow Countrymen,--The entrance of our own beloved country into the grim and terrible war for democracy and human rights which has shaken the world creates so many problems of national life and action which call for immediate consideration and settlement that I hope you will permit me to address to you a few words of earnest counsel and appeal with regard to them.

We are rapidly putting our navy upon an effective war footing and are about to create and equip a great army, but these are the simplest parts of the great task to which we have addressed ourselves. There is not a single selfish element, so far as I can see, in the cause we are fighting for. We are fighting for what we believe and wish to be the rights of mankind and for the future peace and security of the world. To do this great thing worthily and successfully we must devote ourselves to the service without regard to profit or material advantage 33and with an energy and intelligence that will rise to the level of the enterprise itself. We must realize to the full how great the task is and how many things, how many kinds and elements of capacity and service and self-sacrifice it involves.

WHAT WE MUST DO

These, then, are the things we must do, and do well, besides fighting--the things without which mere fighting would be fruitless:

We must supply abundant food for ourselves and for our armies and our seamen, not only, but also for a large part of the nations with whom we have now made common cause, in whose support and by whose sides we shall be fighting.

We must supply ships by the hundreds out of our shipyards to carry to the other side of the sea, submarines or no submarines, what will every day be needed there, and abundant materials out of our fields and our mines and our factories with which not only to clothe and equip our own forces on land and sea, but also to clothe and support our people, for whom the gallant fellows under arms can no longer work; to help clothe and equip the armies with which we are co-operating in Europe, and to keep the looms and manufactories there in raw material; coal to keep the fires going in ships at sea and in the furnaces 34of hundreds of factories across the sea; steel out of which to make arms and ammunition both here and there; rails for wornout railways back of the fighting fronts; locomotives and rolling-stock to take the place of those every day going to pieces; mules, horses, cattle for labor and for military service; everything with which the people of England and France and Italy and Russia have usually supplied themselves, but cannot now afford the men, the materials or the machinery to make.

GREATER EFFICIENCY

It is evident to every thinking man that our industries, on the farms, in the shipyards, in the mines, in the factories, must be made more prolific and more efficient than ever, and that they must be more economically managed and better adapted to the particular requirements of our task than they have been; and what I want to say is that the men and the women who devote their thought and their energy to these things will be serving the country and conducting the fight for peace and freedom just as truly and just as effectively as the men on the battle-field or in the trenches. The industrial forces of the country, men and women alike, will be a great national, a great international, service army--a notable and honored host engaged in the service of the nation and the world, the efficient friends and saviors of 35free men everywhere. Thousands, nay, hundreds of thousands, of men otherwise liable to military service will of right and of necessity be excused from that service and assigned to the fundamental sustaining work of the fields and factories and mines, and they will be as much part of the great patriotic forces of the nation as the men under fire.

I take the liberty, therefore, of addressing this word to the farmers of the country and to all who work on the farms: The supreme need of our own nation and of the nations with which we are co-operating is an abundance of supplies, and especially of foodstuffs. The importance of an adequate food-supply, especially for the present year, is superlative. Without abundant food, alike for the armies and the peoples now at war, the whole great enterprise upon which we have embarked will break down and fail. The world's food reserves are low. Not only during the present emergency, but for some time after peace shall have come, both our own people and a large proportion of the people of Europe must rely upon the harvests in America.

THE RESPONSIBILITY OF THE FARMERS

Upon the farmers of this country, therefore, in large measure rest the fate of the war and the fate of the nations. May the nation not count upon them to omit no step that will 36increase the production of their land or that will bring about the most effectual co-operation in the sale and distribution of their products? The time is short. It is of the most imperative importance that everything possible be done, and done immediately, to make sure of large harvests. I call upon young men and old alike and upon the able-bodied boys of the land to accept and act upon this duty--to turn in hosts to the farms and make certain that no pains and no labor is lacking in this great matter.

I particularly appeal to the farmers of the South to plant abundant foodstuffs, as well as cotton. They can show their patriotism in no better or more convincing way than by resisting the great temptation of the present price of cotton and helping, helping upon a great scale, to feed the nation and the peoples everywhere who are fighting for their liberties and for our own. The variety of their crops will be the visible measure of their comprehension of their national duty.

The Government of the United States and the Governments of the several States stand ready to co-operate. They will do everything possible to assist farmers in securing an adequate supply of seed, an adequate force of laborers when they are most needed, at harvest-time, and the means of expediting shipments of fertilizers and farm machinery, as well as 37of the crops themselves when harvested. The course of trade shall be as unhampered as it is possible to make it, and there shall be no unwarranted manipulation of the nation's food-supply by those who handle it on its way to the consumer. This is our opportunity to demonstrate the efficiency of a great democracy, and we shall not fall short of it!

THE DUTY OF MIDDLEMEN

This let me say to the middlemen of every sort, whether they are handling our foodstuffs or the raw materials of manufacture or the products of our mills and factories: The eyes of the country will be especially upon you. This is your opportunity for signal service, efficient and disinterested. The country expects you, as it expects all others, to forego unusual profits, to organize and expedite shipments of supplies of every kind, but especially of food, with an eye to the service you are rendering and in the spirit of those who enlist in the ranks, for their people, not for themselves. I shall confidently expect you to deserve and win the confidence of people of every sort and station.

THE MEN OF THE RAILWAYS

To the men who run the railways of the country, whether they be managers or operative employees, let me say that the railways are 38the arteries of the nation's life and that upon them rests the immense responsibility of seeing to it that those arteries suffer no obstruction of any kind, no inefficiency or slackened power. To the merchant let me suggest the motto, "Small profits and quick service," and to the shipbuilder the thought that the life of the war depends upon him. The food and the war supplies must be carried across the seas, no matter how many ships are sent to the bottom. The places of those that go down must be supplied, and supplied at once. To the miner let me say that he stands where the farmer does: the work of the world waits on him. If he slackens or fails, armies and statesmen are helpless. He also is enlisted in the great Service Army. The manufacturer does not need to be told, I hope, that the nation looks to him to speed and perfect every process; and I want only to remind his employees that their service is absolutely indispensable and is counted on by every man who loves the country and its liberties.

Let me suggest also that every one who creates or cultivates a garden helps, and helps greatly, to solve the problem of the feeding of the nations; and that every housewife who practises strict economy puts herself in the ranks of those who serve the nation. This is the time for America to correct her unpardonable fault of wastefulness and extravagance. 39Let every man and every woman assume the duty of careful, provident use and expenditure as a public duty, as a dictate of patriotism which no one can now expect ever to be excused or forgiven for ignoring.

THE SUPREME TEST

In the hope that this statement of the needs of the nation and of the world in this hour of supreme crisis may stimulate those to whom it comes and remind all who need reminder of the solemn duties of a time such as the world has never seen before, I beg that all editors and publishers everywhere will give as prominent publication and as wide circulation as possible to this appeal. I venture to suggest also to all advertising agencies that they would perhaps render a very substantial and timely service to the country if they would give it widespread repetition. And I hope that clergymen will not think the theme of it an unworthy or inappropriate subject of comment and homily from their pulpits.

The supreme test of the nation has come. We must all speak, act and serve together.

V

THE CONSCRIPTION PROCLAMATION

(May 18, 1917)

Whereas, Congress has enacted and the President has on the 18th day of May, 1917, approved a law which contains the following provisions:

Section 5. That all male persons between the ages of twenty-one and thirty, both inclusive, shall be subject to registration in accordance with regulations to be prescribed by the President, and upon proclamation by the President or other public notice given by him or by his direction, stating the time and place of such registration, it shall be the duty of all persons of the designated ages, except officers and enlisted men of the Regular Army, the Navy and the National Guard and Naval Militia while in the service of the United States, to present themselves for and submit to registration under the provisions of this act.

And every such person shall be deemed to have notice of the requirements of this act upon the publication of said proclamation or 41other notice as aforesaid given by the President or by his direction.

THE PENALTY FOR FAILURE

And any person who shall wilfully fail or refuse to present himself for registration or to submit thereto as herein provided, shall be guilty of a misdemeanor and shall, upon conviction in the District Court of the United States having jurisdiction thereof, be punished by imprisonment for not more than one year, and shall thereupon be duly registered.

Provided, that in the call of the docket preference shall be given, in courts trying the same, to the trial of criminal proceedings under this act.

Provided, further, that persons shall be subject to registration as herein provided who shall have attained their twenty-first birthday and who shall not have attained their thirty-first birthday on or before the day set for the registration, and all persons so registered shall be and remain subject to draft into the forces hereby authorized unless exempted or excused therefrom, as in this act provided.

Provided, further, that in the case of temporary absence from actual place of legal residence of any person liable to registration as provided herein, such registration may be made by mail under regulations to be prescribed by the President.

42

THE WORK OF REGISTRATION

Section 6. That the President is hereby authorized to utilize the service of any or all departments and any or all officers or agents of the United States and of the several States, Territories and the District of Columbia and subdivisions thereof, in the execution of this act, and all officers and agents of the United States and of the several States, Territories and subdivisions thereof, and of the District of Columbia, and all persons designated or appointed under regulations prescribed by the President, whether such appointments are made by the President himself or by the Governor or other officer of any State or Territory to perform any duty in the execution of this act, are hereby required to perform such duty as the President shall order or direct, and all such officers and agents and persons so designated or appointed shall hereby have full authority for all acts done by them in the execution of this act, by the direction of the President. Correspondence in the execution of this act may be carried in penalty envelopes bearing the frank of the War Department.

44

NEGLECT OF DUTY AND FRAUD

Any person charged, as herein provided, with the duty of carrying into effect any of the provisions of this act or the regulations made or 43directions given thereunder who shall fail or neglect to perform such duty, and any person charged with such duty or having and exercising any authority under said act, regulations or directions, who shall knowingly make or be a party to the making of any false or incorrect registration, physical examination, exemption, enlistment, enrolment or muster.

And any person who shall make or be a party to the making of any false statement or certificate as to the fitness or liability of himself or any other person for service under the provisions of this act, or regulations made by the President thereunder, or otherwise evades or aids another to evade the requirements of this act or of said regulations, or who, in any manner, shall fail or neglect fully to perform any duty required of him in the execution of this act, shall, if not subject to military law, be guilty of a misdemeanor and upon conviction in the District Court of the United States having jurisdiction thereof be punished by imprisonment for not more than one year, or, if subject to military law, shall be tried by court martial and suffer such punishment as a court martial may direct.

A CALL TO GOVERNORS

Now, therefore, I, Woodrow Wilson, President of the United States, do call upon the Governor of each of the several States and 44Territories, the Board of Commissioners of the District of Columbia and all officers and agents of the several States and Territories, of the District of Columbia, and of the counties and municipalities therein, to perform certain duties in the execution of the foregoing law, which duties will be communicated to them directly in regulations of even date herewith.

And I do further proclaim and give notice to all persons subject to registration in the several States and in the District of Columbia, in accordance with the above law, that the time and place of such registration shall be between 7 A.M. and 7 P.M. on the 5th day of June, 1917, at the registration place in the precinct wherein they have their permanent homes.

Those who shall have attained their twenty-first birthday and who shall not have attained their thirty-first birthday on or before the day here named are required to register, excepting only officers and enlisted men of the Regular Army, the Navy, the Marine Corps and the National Guard and Naval Militia while in the service of the United States, and officers in the Officers' Reserve Corps and enlisted men in the enlisted Reserve Corps while in active service. In the Territories of Alaska, Hawaii and Porto Rico a day for registration will be named in a later proclamation.

45

REGISTRATION BY MAIL

And I do hereby charge those who, through sickness, shall be unable to present themselves for registration that they apply on or before the day of registration to the County Clerk of the county where they may be for instructions as to how they may be registered by agent.

Those who expect to be absent on the day named from the counties in which they have their permanent homes may register by mail, but their mailed registration cards must reach the places in which they have their permanent homes by the day named herein. They should apply as soon as practicable to the County Clerk of the county wherein they may be for instructions as to how they may accomplish their registration by mail.

In case such persons as, through sickness or absence, may be unable to present themselves personally for registration shall be sojourning in cities of over 30,000 population, they shall apply to the City Clerk of the city wherein they may be sojourning rather than to the Clerk of the county.

The Clerks of counties and of cities of over 30,000 population, in which numerous applications from the sick and from non-residents are expected, are authorized to establish such sub-agencies and to employ and deputize such clerical 46force as may be necessary to accommodate these applications.

THE WHOLE NATION AN ARMY

The Power against which we are arrayed has sought to impose its will upon the world by force. To this end it has increased armament until it has changed the face of war. In the sense in which we have been wont to think of armies there are no armies in this struggle, there are entire nations armed.

Thus, the men who remain to till the soil and man the factories are no less a part of the army that is in France than the men beneath the battle flags.

It must be so with us. It is not an army that we must shape and train for war--it is a Nation. To this end our people must draw close in one compact front against a common foe. But this cannot be if each man pursues a private purpose. All must pursue one purpose. The Nation needs all men, but it needs each man, not in the field that will most pleasure him, but in the endeavor that will best serve the common good.

Thus, though a sharpshooter pleases to operate a trip-hammer for the forging of great guns, and an expert machinist desires to march with the flag, the Nation is being served only when the sharpshooter marches and the machinist remains at his levers. The whole Nation 47must be a team, in which each man shall play the part for which he is best fitted.

NOT A DRAFT OF THE UNWILLING

To this end Congress has provided that the Nation shall be organized for war by selection, that each man shall be classified for service in the place to which it shall best serve the general good to call him.

The significance of this cannot be overstated. It is a new thing in our history and a landmark in our progress. It is a new manner of accepting and vitalizing our duty to give ourselves with thoughtful devotion to the common purpose of us all. It is in no sense a conscription of the unwilling. It is, rather, selection from a Nation which has volunteered in mass.

It is no more a choosing of those who shall march with the colors than it is a selection of those who shall serve an equally necessary and devoted purpose in the industries that lie behind the battle-lines.

The day here named is the time upon which all shall present themselves for assignment to their tasks. It is for that reason destined to be remembered as one of the most conspicuous moments in our history. It is nothing less than the day upon which the manhood of the country shall step forward in one solid rank in defense of the ideals to which this Nation is consecrated. It is important to those ideals, 48no less than to the pride of this generation in manifesting its devotion to them, that there be no gaps in the ranks.

DAY OF PATRIOTIC DEVOTION

It is essential that the day be approached in thoughtful apprehension of its significance and that we accord to it the honor and the meaning that it deserves. Our industrial need prescribes that it be not made a technical holiday, but the stern sacrifice that is before us urges that it be carried in all our hearts as a great day of patriotic devotion and obligation, when the duty shall lie upon every man, whether he is himself to be registered or not, to see to it that the name of every male person of the designated ages is written on these lists of honor.

In witness whereof, I have hereunto set my hand and caused the seal of the United States to be affixed.

Done at the city of Washington this 18th day of May, in the year of our Lord, 1917, and of the independence of the United States of America the one hundred and forty-first.

By the President: Robert Lansing,
Secretary of State.

49

VI

CONSERVING THE NATION'S FOOD

(May 19, 1917)

It is very desirable, in order to prevent misunderstanding or alarms and to assure co-operation in a vital matter, that the country should understand exactly the scope and purpose of the very great powers which I have thought it necessary, in the circumstances, to ask the Congress to put in my hands with regard to our food-supplies.

Those powers are very great, indeed, but they are no greater than it has proved necessary to lodge in the other Governments which are conducting this momentous war, and their object is stimulation and conservation, not arbitrary restraint or injurious interference with the normal processes of production. They are intended to benefit and assist the farmer and all those who play a legitimate part in the preparation, distribution and marketing of foodstuffs.

A SHARP LINE OF DISTINCTION

It is proposed to draw a sharp line of distinction between the normal activities of the 50Government, represented in the Department of Agriculture, in reference to food production, conservation and marketing, on the one hand, and the emergency activities necessitated by the war, in reference to the regulation of food distribution and consumption, on the other.

All measures intended directly to extend the normal activities of the Department of Agriculture, in reference to the production, conservation and the marketing of farm crops, will be administered, as in normal times, through that department; and the powers asked for over distribution and consumption, over exports, imports, prices, purchase and requisition of commodities, storing and the like, which may require regulation during the war, will be placed in the hands of a Commissioner of Food Administration, appointed by the President and directly responsible to him.

THE END TO BE ATTAINED

The objects sought to be served by the legislation asked for are: Full inquiry into the existing available stocks of foodstuffs and into the costs and practices of the various food producing and distributing trades; the prevention of all unwarranted hoarding of every kind, and of the control of foodstuffs by persons who are not in any legitimate sense producers, dealers or traders; the requisition, when necessary for public use, of food supplies and of the equipment 51necessary for handling them properly; the licensing of wholesome and legitimate mixtures and milling percentages, and the prohibition of the unnecessary or wasteful use of foods.

Authority is asked also to establish prices, but not in order to limit the profits of the farmers, but only to guarantee to them, when necessary, a minimum price, which will insure them a profit where they are asked to attempt new crops, and to secure the consumer against extortion by breaking up corners and attempts at speculation when they occur, by fixing temporarily a reasonable price at which middlemen must sell.

THE FIXING OF PRICES

I have asked Mr. Herbert Hoover to undertake this all-important task of food administration. He has expressed his willingness to do so, on condition that he is to receive no payment for his services, and that the whole of the force under him, exclusive of clerical assistance, shall be employed, as far as possible, upon the same volunteer basis.

He has expressed his confidence that this difficult matter of food administration can be successfully accomplished through the voluntary co-operation and direction of legitimate distributers of food-stuffs and with the help of the women of the country.

52

Although it is absolutely necessary that unquestionable powers shall be placed in my hands, in order to insure the success of this administration of the food-supplies of the country, I am confident that the exercise of those powers will be necessary only in the few cases where some small and selfish minority proves unwilling to put the Nation's interests above personal advantage, and that the whole country will heartily support Mr. Hoover's efforts by supplying the necessary volunteer agencies throughout the country for the intelligent control of food consumption, and securing the co-operation of the most capable leaders of the very interests most directly affected, that the exercise of the powers deputed to him will rest very successfully upon the good-will and co-operation of the people themselves, and that the ordinary economic machinery of the country will be left substantially undisturbed.

NO FEAR OF BUREAUCRACY

The proposed food administration is intended, of course, only to meet a manifest emergency and to continue only while the war lasts. Since it will be composed for the most part of volunteers, there need be no fear of the possibility of a permanent bureaucracy arising out of it.

All control of consumption will disappear when the emergency has passed. It is with that object in view that the Administration 53considers it to be of pre-eminent importance that the existing associations of producers and distributers of foodstuffs should be mobilized and made use of on a volunteer basis. The successful conduct of the projected food administration, by such means, will be the finest possible demonstration of the willingness, the ability and the efficiency of democracy and of its justified reliance upon the freedom of individual initiative.

The last thing that any American could contemplate with equanimity would be the introduction of anything resembling Prussian autocracy into the food control of this country.

It is of vital interest and importance to every man who produces food and to every man who takes part in its distribution that these policies, thus liberally administered, should succeed and succeed altogether. It is only in that way that we can prove it to be absolutely unnecessary to resort to the rigorous and drastic measures which have proved to be necessary in some of the European countries.

54

VII

AN ANSWER TO CRITICS

(May 22, 1917)

In the following letter, addressed to Representative Heflin, Democrat, of Alabama, President Wilson replies to criticisms regarding his position with regard to the war and its objects:

It is incomprehensible to me how any frank or honest person could doubt or question my position with regard to the war and its objects. I have again and again stated the very serious and long-continued wrongs which the Imperial German Government has perpetrated against the rights, the commerce and the citizens of the United States. The list is long and overwhelming. No Nation that respected itself or the rights of humanity could have borne those wrongs any longer.

Our objects in going into the war have been stated with equal clearness. The whole of the conception which I take to be the conception of our fellow-countrymen with regard to the outcome of the war and the terms of its settlement, I set forth with the utmost explicitness 55in an address to the Senate of the United States on the 22d of January last. Again, in my message to Congress on the 2d of April last, those objects were stated in unmistakable terms.

I can conceive no purpose in seeking to becloud this matter except the purpose of weakening the hands of the Government and making the part which the United States is to play in this great struggle for human liberty an inefficient and hesitating part.

We have entered the war for our own reasons and with our own objects clearly stated, and shall forget neither the reasons nor the objects. There is no hate in our hearts for the German people, but there is a resolve which cannot be shaken even by misrepresentation, to overcome the pretensions of the autocratic Government which acts upon purposes to which the German people have never consented.

56

VIII

MEMORIAL DAY ADDRESS

(May 30, 1917)

In one sense the great struggle into which we have now entered is an American struggle, because it is in defense of American honor and American rights, but it is something even greater than that; it is a world struggle. It is the struggle of men who love liberty everywhere, and in this cause America will show herself greater than ever because she will rise to a greater thing.

The program has conferred an unmerited dignity upon the remarks I am going to make by calling them an address, because I am not here to deliver an address [said the President]. I am here merely to show in my official capacity the sympathy of this great Government with the object of this occasion, and also to speak just a word of the sentiment that is in my own heart.

Any memorial day of this sort is, of course, a day touched with sorrowful memory, and yet I for one do not see how we can have any 57thought of pity for the men whose memory we honor to-day. I do not pity them. I envy them, rather, because their great work for liberty is accomplished, and we are in the midst of a work unfinished, testing our strength where their strength already has been tested.

A HERITAGE FROM THE DEAD

There is a touch of sorrow, but there is a touch of reassurance also in a day like this, because we know how the men of America have responded to the call of the cause of liberty, and it fills our mind with a perfect assurance that that response will come again in equal measures, with equal majesty and with a result which will hold the attention of all mankind.

When you reflect upon it, these men who died to preserve the Union died to preserve the instrument which we are now using to serve the world--a free nation espousing the cause of human liberty. In one sense the great struggle into which we have now entered is an American struggle, because it is in the sense of American honor and American rights, but it is something even greater than that; it is a world struggle. It is a struggle of men who love liberty everywhere; and in this cause America will show herself greater than ever because she will rise to a greater thing.

We have said in the beginning that we planned this great Government that men who 58wish freedom might have a place of refuge and a place where their hope could be realized, and now, having established such a Government, having preserved such a Government, having vindicated the power of such a Government, we are saying to all mankind, "We did not set this Government up in order that we might have a selfish and separate liberty, for we are now ready to come to your assistance and fight out upon the fields of the world the cause of human liberty."

AMERICA'S FULL FRUITION

In this thing America attains her full dignity and the full fruition of her great purpose.

No man can be glad that such things have happened as we have witnessed in these last fateful years, but perhaps it may be permitted to us to be glad that we have an opportunity to show the principles which we profess to be living--principles which live in our hearts--and to have a chance by the pouring out of our blood and treasure to vindicate the things which we have professed. For, my friends, the real fruition of life is to do the things we have said we wished to do. There are times when words seem empty and only action seems great. Such a time has come, and in the providence of God America will once more have an opportunity to show to the world that she was born to serve mankind.

IX

A STATEMENT TO RUSSIA

(June 9, 1917)

In view of the approaching visit of the American delegation to Russia to express the deep friendship of the American people for the people of Russia and to discuss the best and most practical means of co-operation between the two peoples in carrying the present struggle for the freedom of all peoples to a successful consummation, it seems opportune and appropriate that I should state again, in the light of this new partnership, the objects the United States has had in mind in entering the war. Those objects have been very much beclouded during the past few weeks by mistaken and misleading statements, and the issues at stake are too momentous, too tremendous, too significant for the whole human race to permit any misinterpretations or misunderstandings, however slight, to remain uncorrected for a moment.

The war has begun to go against Germany, and in their desperate desire to escape the 60inevitable ultimate defeat, those who are in authority in Germany are using every possible instrumentality, are making use even of the influence of groups and parties among their own subjects to whom they have never been just or fair, or even tolerant, to promote a propaganda on both sides of the sea which will preserve for them their influence at home and their power abroad, to the undoing of the very men they are using.

AMERICA SEEKS NO CONQUEST

The position of America in this war is so clearly avowed that no man can be excused for mistaking it. She seeks no material profit or aggrandizement of any kind. She is fighting for no advantage or selfish object of her own, but for the liberation of peoples everywhere from the aggressions of autocratic force. The ruling classes in Germany have begun of late to profess a like liberality and justice of purpose, but only to preserve the power they have set up in Germany and the selfish advantages which they have wrongly gained for themselves and their private projects of power all the way from Berlin to Bagdad and beyond. Government after Government has, by their influence, without open conquest of its territory, been linked together in a net of intrigue directed against nothing less than the peace and liberty of the world. The meshes of that 61intrigue must be broken, but cannot be broken unless wrongs already done are undone; and adequate measures must be taken to prevent it from ever again being rewoven or repaired.

Of course the Imperial German Government and those whom it is using for their own undoing are seeking to obtain pledges that the war will end in the restoration of the *status quo ante*. It was the *status quo ante* out of which this iniquitous war issued forth, the power of the Imperial German Government within the empire and its widespread domination and influence outside of that empire. That status must be altered in such fashion as to prevent any such hideous thing from ever happening again.

THE PRINCIPLES THAT ARE INVOLVED

We are fighting for the liberty, self-government and the undictated development of all peoples, and every feature of the settlement that concludes this war must be conceived and executed for that purpose. Wrongs must first be righted and then adequate safeguards must be created to prevent their being committed again. We ought not to consider remedies merely because they have a pleasing and sonorous sound. Practical questions can be settled only by practical means. Phrases will not accomplish the result. Effective readjustments will; and whatever readjustments are necessary must be made.

62

But they must follow a principle, and that principle is plain:

No people must be forced under sovereignty under which it does not wish to live.

No territory must change hands except for the purpose of securing those who inhabit it a fair chance of life and liberty.

No indemnities must be insisted on except those that constitute payment for manifest wrongs done.

No readjustments of power must be made except such as will tend to secure the future peace of the world and the future welfare and happiness of its peoples.

And then the free peoples of the world must draw together in some common covenant, some genuine and practical co-operation, that will in effect combine their force to secure peace and justice in the dealings of nations with one another. The brotherhood of mankind must no longer be a fair but empty phrase; it must be given a structure of force and reality. The nations must realize their common life and effect a workable partnership to secure that life against the aggressions of autocratic and self-pleasing power.

For these things we can afford to pour out blood and treasure. For these are the things we have always professed to desire, and unless we pour out blood and treasure now and succeed, we may never be able to unite or show 63conquering force again in the great cause of human liberty. The day has come to conquer or submit. If the forces of autocracy can divide us, they will overcome us; if we stand together, victory is certain and the liberty which victory will secure.

We can afford, then, to be generous, but we cannot afford then or now to be weak or omit any single guarantee of justice and security.

64

X

FLAG-DAY ADDRESS

(June 14, 1917)

My Fellow-citizens,--We meet to celebrate Flag Day because this flag which we honor and under which we serve is the emblem of our unity, our power, our thought and purpose as a nation. It has no other character than that which we give it from generation to generation. The choices are ours. It floats in majestic silence above the hosts that execute those choices, whether in peace or in war. And yet, though silent, it speaks to us--speaks to us of the past, of the men and women who went before us and of the records they wrote upon it. We celebrate the day of its birth; and from its birth until now it has witnessed a great history, has floated on high the symbol of great events, of a great plan of life worked out by a great people. We are about to carry it into battle, to lift it where it will draw the fire of our enemies. We are about to bid thousands, hundreds of thousands, it may be millions, of our men--the young, the strong, 65the capable men of the nation--to go forth and die beneath it on fields of blood far away--for what? For some unaccustomed thing? For something for which it has never sought the fire before? American armies were never before sent across the seas. Why are they sent now? For some new purpose, for which this great flag has never been carried before, or for some old, familiar, heroic purpose for which it has seen men, its own men, die on every battlefield upon which Americans have borne arms since the Revolution?

These are questions which must be answered. We are Americans. We in our turn serve America, and can serve her with no private purpose. We must use her flag as she has always used it. We are accountable at the bar of history and must plead in utter frankness what purpose it is we seek to serve.

WHY WE ARE AT WAR

It is plain enough how we were forced into the war. The extraordinary insults and aggressions of the Imperial German Government left us no self-respecting choice but to take up arms in defense of our rights as a free people and of our honor as a sovereign Government. The military masters of Germany denied us the right to be neutral. They filled our unsuspecting communities with vicious spies and conspirators and sought to corrupt the opinion 66of our people in their own behalf. When they found that they could not do that, their agents diligently spread sedition among us and sought to draw our own citizens from their allegiance--and some of those agents were men connected with the official embassy of the German Government itself here in our own capital. They sought by violence to destroy our own industries and arrest our commerce. They tried to incite Mexico to take up arms against us and to draw Japan into a hostile alliance with her--and that, not by indirection, but by direct suggestion from the Foreign Office in Berlin. They impudently denied us the use of the seas and repeatedly executed their threat that they would send to their death any of our people who ventured to approach the coasts of Europe. And many of our own people were corrupted. Men began to look upon their own neighbors with suspicion and to wonder, in their hot resentment and surprise, whether there was any community in which hostile intrigue did not lurk. What great nation, in such circumstances, would not have taken up arms? Much as we had desired peace, it was denied us, and not of our own choice. This flag under which we serve would have been dishonored had we withheld our hand.

But that is only part of the story. We know now as clearly as we knew before we were ourselves engaged that we are not the 67enemies of the German people and that they are not our enemies. They did not originate or desire this hideous war or wish that we should be drawn into it; and we are vaguely conscious that we are fighting their cause, as they will some day see it, as well as our own. They are themselves in the grip of the same sinister power that has now at last stretched its ugly talons out and drawn blood from us.

The whole world is at war because the whole world is in the grip of that power and is trying out the great battle which shall determine whether it is to be brought under its mastery or fling itself free.

THE RESPONSIBILITY FOR THE CONFLICT

The war was begun by the military masters of Germany, who proved to be also the masters of Austria-Hungary. These men have never regarded nations as peoples, men, women and children of like blood and frame as themselves, for whom governments existed and in whom governments had their life. They have regarded them merely as serviceable organizations which they could by force or intrigue bend or corrupt to their own purpose. They have regarded the smaller states, in particular, and the peoples who could be overwhelmed by force, as their natural tools and instruments of domination. Their purpose has long been avowed. The statesmen of other nations, to 68whom that purpose was incredible, paid little attention; regarded what German professors expounded in their class-rooms and German writers set forth to the world as the goal of German policy as rather the dream of minds detached from practical affairs, as preposterous private conceptions of German destiny, than as the actual plans of responsible rulers; but the rulers of Germany themselves knew all the while what concrete plans, what well-advanced intrigues, lay back of what the professors and the writers were saying, and were glad to go forward unmolested, filling the thrones of Balkan states with German princes, putting German officers at the service of Turkey to drill her armies and make interest with her Government, developing plans of sedition and rebellion in India and Egypt, setting their fires in Persia. The demands made by Austria upon Serbia were a mere single step in a plan which compassed Europe and Asia, from Berlin to Bagdad. They hoped those demands might not arouse Europe, but they meant to press them whether they did or not, for they thought themselves ready for the final issue of arms.

THE PLAN OF CONQUEST

Their plan was to throw a broad belt of German military power and political control across the very center of Europe and beyond the Mediterranean into the very heart of Asia; and 69Austria-Hungary was to be as much their tool and pawn as Serbia or Bulgaria or Turkey or the ponderous states of the East. Austria-Hungary, indeed, was to become part of the central German Empire, absorbed and dominated by the same forces and influences that had originally cemented the German states themselves. The dream had its heart at Berlin. It could have had a heart nowhere else! It rejected the idea of solidarity of race entirely. The choice of peoples played no part in it at all. It contemplated binding together racial and political units which could be kept together only by force--Czechs, Magyars, Croats, Serbs, Rumanians, Turks, Armenians--the proud states of Bohemia and Hungary, the stout little commonwealths of the Balkans, the indomitable Turks, the subtile peoples of the East. These peoples did not wish to be united. They ardently desired to direct their own affairs, would be satisfied only by undisputed independence. They could be kept quiet only by the presence or the constant threat of armed men. They would live under a common power only by sheer compulsion and await the day of revolution. But the German military statesmen had reckoned with all that and were ready to deal with it in their own way.

And they have actually carried the greater part of that amazing plan into execution! Look how things stand. Austria is at their mercy. 70It has acted, not upon its own initiative or upon the choice of its own people, but at Berlin's dictation, ever since the war began. Its people now desire peace, but cannot have it until leave is granted from Berlin. The so-called Central Powers are, in fact, but a single Power. Serbia is at its mercy, should its hand be but for a moment freed. Bulgaria has consented to its will, and Rumania is overrun. The Turkish armies, which Germans trained, are serving Germany, certainly not themselves, and the guns of German warships lying in the harbor at Constantinople remind Turkish statesmen every day that they have no choice but to take their orders from Berlin. From Hamburg to the Persian Gulf the net is spread.

THE TALK OF PEACE

Is it not easy to understand the eagerness for peace that has been manifested from Berlin ever since the snare was set and sprung? Peace, peace, peace has been the talk of her Foreign Office for now a year and more; not peace upon her own initiative, but upon the initiative of the nations over which she now deems herself to hold the advantage. A little of the talk has been public, but most of it has been private. Through all sorts of channels it has come to me, and in all sorts of guises, but never with the terms disclosed which the German 71Government would be willing to accept. That Government has other valuable pawns in its hands besides those I have mentioned. It still holds a valuable part of France, though with slowly relaxing grasp, and practically the whole of Belgium. Its armies press close upon Russia and overrun Poland at their will. It cannot go farther; it dare not go back. It wishes to close its bargain before it is too late, and it has little left to offer for the pound of flesh it will demand.

The military masters under whom Germany is bleeding see very clearly to what point Fate has brought them. If they fall back or are forced back an inch, their power both abroad and at home will fall to pieces like a house of cards. It is their power at home they are thinking about now more than their power abroad. It is that power which is trembling under their very feet; and deep fear has entered their hearts. They have but one chance to perpetuate their military power, or even their controlling political influence. If they can secure peace now, with the immense advantages still in their hands which they have up to this point apparently gained, they will have justified themselves before the German people; they will have gained by force what they promised to gain by it--an immense expansion of German power, an immense enlargement of German industrial and commercial opportunities. 72Their prestige will be secure, and with their prestige their political power. If they fail, their people will thrust them aside; a government accountable to the people themselves will be set up in Germany, as it has been in England, in the United States, in France, and in all the great countries of the modern time except Germany. If they succeed they are safe and Germany and the world are undone; if they fail Germany is saved and the world will be at peace. If they succeed, America will fall within the menace. We and all the rest of the world must remain armed, as they will remain, and must make ready for the next step in their aggression; if they fail, the world may unite for peace and Germany may be of the union.

THE PRESENT AIM OF GERMANY

Do you not now understand the new intrigue, the intrigue for peace, and why the masters of Germany do not hesitate to use any agency that promises to effect their purpose, the deceit of the nations? Their present particular aim is to deceive all those who throughout the world stand for the rights of peoples and the self-government of nations; for they see what immense strength the forces of justice and of liberalism are gathering out of this war. They are employing liberals in their enterprise. They are using men, in Germany and without, as 73their spokesmen whom they have hitherto despised and oppressed, using them for their own destruction--socialists, the leaders of labor, the thinkers they have hitherto sought to silence. Let them once succeed and these men, now their tools, will be ground to powder beneath the weight of the great military empire they will have set up; the revolutionists in Russia will be cut off from all succor or co-operation in western Europe and a counter revolution fostered and supported; Germany herself will lose her chance of freedom; and all Europe will arm for the next, the final struggle.

The sinister intrigue is being no less actively conducted in this country than in Russia, and in every country in Europe to which the agents and dupes of the Imperial German Government can get access. That Government has many spokesmen here, in places high and low. They have learned discretion. They keep within the law. It is opinion they utter now, not sedition. They proclaim the liberal purposes of their masters; declare this a foreign war which can touch America with no danger to either her lands or her institutions; set England at the center of the stage and talk of her ambition to assert economic dominion throughout the world; appeal to our ancient tradition of isolation in the politics of the nations; and seek to undermine the Government with false professions of loyalty to its principles.

74

THIS IS A PEOPLES' WAR

But they will make no headway. The false betray themselves always in every accent. It is only friends and partisans of the German Government whom we have already identified who utter these thinly disguised disloyalties. The facts are patent to all the world, and nowhere are they more plainly seen than in the United States, where we are accustomed to deal with facts and not with sophistries; and the great fact that stands out above all the rest is that this is a Peoples' War, a war for freedom and justice and self-government amongst all the nations of the world, a war to make the world safe for the peoples who live in it and have made it their own, the German people themselves included; and that with us rests the choice to break through all these hypocrisies and patent cheats and masks of brute force and help set the world free, or else stand aside and let it be dominated a long age through by sheer weight of arms and the arbitrary choices of self-constituted masters, by the nation which can maintain the biggest armies and the most irresistible armaments--a power to which the world has afforded no parallel and in the face of which political freedom must wither and perish.

For us there is but one choice. We have made it. Woe be to the man or group of men 75that seeks to stand in our way in this day of high resolution, when every principle we hold dearest is to be vindicated and made secure for the salvation of the nations. We are ready to plead at the bar of history, and our flag shall wear a new luster. Once more we shall make good with our lives and fortunes the great faith to which we were born, and a new glory shall shine in the face of our people.

XI

AN APPEAL TO THE BUSINESS INTERESTS

(July 11, 1917)

My Fellow-countrymen,--The Government is about to attempt to determine the prices at which it will ask you henceforth to furnish various supplies which are necessary for the prosecution of the war, and various materials which will be needed in the industries by which the war must be sustained.

We shall, of course, try to determine them justly and to the best advantage of the nation as a whole. But justice is easier to speak of than to arrive at, and there are some considerations which I hope we shall keep steadily in mind while this particular problem of justice is being worked out.

I therefore take the liberty of stating very candidly my own view of the situation and of the principles which should guide both the Government and the mine-owners and manufacturers of the country in this difficult matter.

77

PATRIOTISM AND PROFITS APART

A just price must, of course, be paid for everything the Government buys. By a just price I mean a price which will sustain the industries concerned in a high state of efficiency, provide a living for those who conduct them, enable them to pay good wages, and make possible the expansions of their enterprises, which will from time to time become necessary as the stupendous undertakings of this great war develop.

We could not wisely or reasonably do less than pay such prices. They are necessary for the maintenance and development of industry; and the maintenance and development of industry are necessary for the great task we have in hand.

But I trust that we shall not surround the matter with a mist of sentiment. Facts are our masters now. We ought not to put the acceptance of such prices on the ground of patriotism. Patriotism has nothing to do with profits in a case like this. Patriotism and profits ought never in the present circumstances to be mentioned together.

It is perfectly proper to discuss profits as a matter of business, with a view to maintaining the integrity of capital and the efficiency of labor in these tragical months, when the liberty of free men everywhere and of industry 78itself trembles in the balance, but it would be absurd to discuss them as a motive for helping to serve and save our country.

Patriotism leaves profits out of the question. In these days of our supreme trial, when we are sending hundreds of thousands of our young men across the seas to serve a great cause, no true man who stays behind to work for them and sustain them by his labor will ask himself what he is personally going to make out of that labor.

No true patriot will permit himself to take toll of their heroism in money or seek to grow rich by the shedding of their blood. He will give as freely and with as unstinted self-sacrifice as they. When they are giving their lives, will he not at least give his money?

I hear it insisted that more than a just price, more than a price that will sustain our industries, must be paid; that it is necessary to pay very liberal and unusual profits in order to "stimulate production," that nothing but pecuniary rewards will do--rewards paid in money, not in the mere liberation of the world.

IS A BRIBE NECESSARY?

I take it for granted that those who argue thus do not stop to think what that means. Do they mean that you must be paid, must be bribed, to make your contribution, a contribution 79that costs you neither a drop of blood, nor a tear, when the whole world is in travail and men everywhere depend upon and call to you to bring them out of bondage and make the world a fit place to live in again amidst peace and justice?

Do they mean that you will exact a price, drive a bargain, with the men who are enduring the agony of this war on the battlefield, in the trenches, amid the lurking dangers of the sea, or with the bereaved women and pitiful children, before you will come forward to do your duty and give some part of your life, in easy, peaceful fashion, for the things we are fighting for, the things we have pledged our fortunes, our lives, our sacred honor, to vindicate and defend-- liberty and justice and fair dealing and the peace of nations?

Of course you will not. It is inconceivable. Your patriotism is of the same self-denying stuff as the patriotism of the men dead or maimed on the fields of France, or else it is no patriotism at all. Let us never speak, then, of profits and of patriotism in the same sentence, but face facts and meet them. Let us do sound business, but not in the midst of a mist.

Many a grievous burden of taxation will be laid on this Nation, in this generation and in the next, to pay for this war; let us see to it that for every dollar that is 80taken from the people's pockets it shall be possible to obtain a dollar's worth of the sound stuffs they need.

HIGH FREIGHTS AID GERMANY

Let us for a moment turn to the ship-owners of the United States and the other ocean carriers whose example they have followed, and ask them if they realize what obstacles, what almost insuperable obstacles, they have been putting in the way of the successful prosecution of this war by the ocean freight rates they have been exacting.

They are doing everything that high freight charges can do to make the war a failure, to make it impossible. I do not say that they realize this or intend it.

The thing has happened naturally enough, because the commercial processes which we are content to see operate in ordinary times have without sufficient thought been continued into a period where they have no proper place. I am not questioning motives. I am merely stating a fact, and stating it in order that attention may be fixed upon it.

The fact is that those who have fixed war freight rates have taken the most effective means in their power to defeat the armies engaged against Germany. When they realize this we may, I take it for granted, count upon them to reconsider the whole matter. It is 81high time. Their extra hazards are covered by war-risk insurance.

THE LAW TO DEAL WITH OFFENDERS

I know, and you know, what response to this great challenge of duty and of opportunity the Nation will expect of you; and I know what response you will make. Those who do not respond, who do not respond in the spirit of those who have gone to give their lives for us on bloody fields far away, may safely be left to be dealt with by opinion and the law--for the law must, of course, command those things.

I am dealing with the matter thus publicly and frankly, not because I have any doubt or fear as to the result, but only in order that, in all our thinking and in all our dealings with one another we may move in a perfectly clear air of mutual understanding.

And there is something more that we must add to our thinking. The public is now as much part of the Government as are the Army and Navy themselves. The whole people, in all their activities, are now mobilized and in service for the accomplishment of the Nation's task in this war. It is in such circumstances impossible justly to distinguish between industrial purchases made by the Government and industries. And it is just as much our duty to sustain the industries of the country, all the 82industries that contribute to its life, as it is to sustain our forces in the field and on the sea. We must make the prices to the public the same as the prices to the Government.

PRICES MEAN VICTORY OR DEFEAT

Prices mean the same thing everywhere now. They mean the efficiency or the inefficiency of the Nation, whether it is the Government that pays them or not. They mean victory or defeat. They mean that America will win her place once for all among the foremost free Nations of the world, or that she will sink to defeat and become a second-rate Power alike in thought and action. This is a day of her reckoning, and every man among us must personally face that reckoning along with her.

The case needs no arguing. I assume that I am only expressing your own thoughts--what must be in the mind of every true man when he faces the tragedy and the solemn glory of the present war, for the emancipation of mankind. I summon you to a great duty, a great privilege, a shining dignity and distinction.

I shall expect every man who is not a slacker to be at my side throughout this great enterprise. In it no man can win honor who thinks of himself.

83

XII

REPLY OF THE UNITED STATES TO THE COMMUNICATION OF THE POPE TO THE BELLIGERENT GOVERNMENTS

(August 27, 1917)

To His Holiness Benedictus XV., Pope.

In acknowledgment of the communication of Your Holiness to the belligerent peoples, dated August 1, 1917, the President of the United States requests me to transmit the following reply:

Every heart that has not been blinded and hardened by this terrible war must be touched by this moving appeal of His Holiness, the Pope, must feel the dignity and force of the humane and generous motives which prompted it, and must fervently wish that we might take the path of peace he so persuasively points out. But it would be folly to take it if it does not, in fact, lead to the goal he proposes. Our response must be based upon the stern facts and upon nothing else. It is not a mere cessation of arms he desires; it is a stable and enduring peace. This agony must not be gone 84through with again, and it must be a matter of very sober judgment what will insure us against it.

THE PROPOSAL FROM THE VATICAN

His Holiness, in substance, proposes that we return to the *status quo ante bellum*, and that then there be a general condonation, disarmament, and a concert of nations based upon an acceptance of the principle of arbitration; that by a similar concert freedom of the seas be established; and that the territorial claims of France and Italy, the perplexing problems of the Balkan states, and the restitution of Poland be left to such conciliatory adjustments as may be possible in the new temper of such a peace, due regard being paid to the aspirations of the peoples whose political fortunes and affiliations will be involved.

It is manifest that no part of this program can be successfully carried out unless the restitution of the *status quo ante* furnishes a firm and satisfactory basis for it. The object of this war is to deliver the free peoples of the world from the menace and the actual power of a vast military establishment controlled by an irresponsible Government, which, having secretly planned to dominate the world, proceeded to carry the plan out without regard either to the sacred obligations of treaty or the long-established practices and long-cherished 85principles of international action and honor; which chose its own time for the war; delivered its blow fiercely and suddenly; stopped at no barrier either of law or of mercy; swept a whole continent within the tide of blood--not the blood of soldiers only, but the blood of innocent women and children also, and of the helpless poor; and now stands balked but not defeated, the enemy of four-fifths of the world. This power is not the German people. It is the ruthless master of the German people. It is no business of ours how that great people came under its control or submitted with temporary zest to the domination of its purpose; but it is our business to see to it that the history of the rest of the world is no longer left to its handling.

To deal with such a power by way of peace upon the plan proposed by His Holiness the Pope would, so far as we can see, involve a recuperation of its strength and a renewal of its policy; would make it necessary to create a permanent hostile combination of nations against the German people who are its instruments; and would result in abandoning the new-born Russia to the intrigue, the manifold subtle interference, and the certain counter-revolution which would be attempted by all the malign influences to which the German Government has of late accustomed the world. Can peace be based upon a restitution of its 86power or upon any word of honor it could pledge in a treaty of settlement and accommodation?

Responsible statesmen must now everywhere see, if they never saw before, that no peace can rest securely upon political or economic restrictions meant to benefit some nations and cripple or embarrass others, upon vindictive action of any sort, or any kind of revenge or deliberate injury. The American people have suffered intolerable wrongs at the hands of the Imperial German Government, but they desire no reprisal upon the German people, who have themselves suffered all things in this war which they did not choose. They believe that peace should rest upon the rights of peoples, not the rights of governments--the rights of peoples great or small, weak or powerful--their equal right to freedom and security and self-government and to a participation upon fair terms in the economic opportunities of the world, the German people, of course, included, if they will accept equality and not seek domination.

The test, therefore, of every plan of peace is this: Is it based upon the faith of all the peoples involved or merely upon the word of an ambitious and intriguing Government on the one hand, and of a group of free peoples on the other? This is a test which goes to the root of the matter; and it is the test which must be applied.

87

THE TEST THAT MUST BE APPLIED

The purposes of the United States in this war are known to the whole world, to every people to whom the truth has been permitted to come. They do not need to be stated again. We seek no material advantage of any kind. We believe that the intolerable wrongs done in this war by the furious and brutal power of the Imperial German Government ought to be repaired, but not at the expense of the sovereignty of any people--rather a vindication of the sovereignty both of those that are weak and of those that are strong. Punitive damages, the dismemberment of empires, the establishment of selfish and exclusive economic leagues, we deem inexpedient and in the end worse than futile, no proper basis for a peace of any kind, least of all for an enduring peace. That must be based upon justice and fairness and the common rights of mankind.

THE GERMAN RULERS CANNOT BE TRUSTED

We cannot take the word of the present rulers of Germany as a guaranty of anything that is to endure, unless explicitly supported by such conclusive evidence of the will and purpose of the German people themselves as the other peoples of the world would be justified in accepting. Without such guarantees treaties of settlement, agreements for disarmament, 88covenants to set up arbitration in the place of force, territorial adjustments, reconstitutions of small nations, if made with the German Government, no man, no nation could now depend on. We must await some new evidence of the purposes of the great peoples of the Central Powers. God grant it may be given soon, and in a way to restore the confidence of all peoples everywhere in the faith of nations and the possibility of a covenanted peace.

Robert Lansing,

Secretary of State of the United States of America.

89

XIII

A MESSAGE TO TEACHERS AND SCHOOL OFFICERS

(September 30, 1917)

The war is bringing to the minds of our people a new appreciation of the problems of national life and a deeper understanding of the meaning and aims of democracy. Matters which heretofore have seemed commonplace and trivial are seen in a truer light. The urgent demand for the production and proper distribution of food and other national resources has made us aware of the close dependence of individual on individual and nation on nation. The effort to keep up social and industrial organizations, in spite of the withdrawal of men for the army, has revealed the extent to which modern life has become complex and specialized.

These and other lessons of the war must be learned quickly if we are intelligently and successfully to defend our institutions. When the war is over 90we must apply the wisdom which we have acquired in purging and ennobling the life of the world.

THE COMMON SCHOOL HAS A PART TO PLAY

In these vital tasks of acquiring a broader view of human possibilities the common school must have large part. I urge that teachers and other school officers increase materially the time and attention devoted to instruction bearing directly on the problems of community and national life.

Such a plea is in no way foreign to the spirit of American public education or of existing practices. Nor is it a plea for a temporary enlargement of the school program appropriate merely to the period of the war. It is a plea for a realization in public education of the new emphasis which the war has given to the ideals of democracy and to the broader conceptions of national life.

In order that there may be definite material at hand with which the schools may at once expand their teachings, I have asked Mr. Hoover and Commissioner Claxton to organize the proper agencies for the preparation and distribution of suitable lessons for the elementary grades and for the high-school classes. Lessons thus suggested will serve the double purpose of illustrating in a concrete way what can be undertaken in the schools and of stimulating 91teachers in all parts of the country to formulate new and appropriate materials drawn directly from the communities in which they live.

Woodrow Wilson.

92

XIV

WOMAN SUFFRAGE MUST COME NOW

(October 25, 1917)

The President received at the White House a delegation from the New York State Woman Suffrage Party. Answering the address made by the chairman, Mrs. Norman de R. Whitehouse, the President spoke as follows:

Mrs. Whitehouse and Ladies,--It is with great pleasure that I receive you. I esteem it a privilege to do so. I know the difficulties which you have been laboring under in New York State, so clearly set forth by Mrs. Whitehouse, but in my judgment those difficulties cannot be used as an excuse by the leaders of any party or by the voters of any party for neglecting the question which you are pressing upon them. Because, after all, the whole world now is witnessing a struggle between two ideals of government. It is a struggle which goes deeper and touches more of the foundations of the organized life of men than any struggle that has ever taken place before, and no settlement of the questions that lie on the 93surface can satisfy a situation which requires that the questions which lie underneath and at the foundation should also be settled and settled right. I am free to say that I think the question of woman suffrage is one of those questions which lie at the foundation.

The world has witnessed a slow political reconstruction, and men have generally been obliged to be satisfied with the slowness of the process. In a sense it is wholesome that it should be slow, because then it is solid and sure. But I believe that this war is going so to quicken the convictions and the consciousness of mankind with regard to political questions that the speed of reconstruction will be greatly increased. And I believe that just because we are quickened by the questions of this war, we ought to be quickened to give this question of woman suffrage our immediate consideration.

NOW IS THE TIME TO ACT

As one of the spokesmen of a great party, I would be doing nothing less than obeying the mandates of that party if I gave my hearty support to the question of woman suffrage which you represent, but I do not want to speak merely as one of the spokesmen of a party. I want to speak for myself, and say that it seems to me that this is the time for the States of this Union to take this action. I 94perhaps may be touched a little too much by the traditions of our politics, traditions which lay such questions almost entirely upon the States, but I want to see communities declare themselves quickened at this time and show the consequence of the quickening.

I think the whole country has appreciated the way in which the women have risen to this great occasion. They not only have done what they have been asked to do, and done it with ardor and efficiency, but they have shown a power to organize for doing things of their own initiative, which is quite a different thing, and a very much more difficult thing, and I think the whole country has admired the spirit and the capacity and the vision of the women of the United States.

It is almost absurd to say that the country depends upon the women for a large part of the inspiration of its life. That is too obvious to say; but it is now depending upon the women also for suggestions of service, which have been rendered in abundance and with the distinction of originality. I, therefore, am very glad to add my voice to those which are urging the people of the great State of New York to set a great example by voting for woman suffrage. It would be a pleasure if I might utter that advice in their presence. Inasmuch as I am bound too close to my duties here to make that possible, I am glad to have the 95privilege to ask you to convey that message to them.

It seems to me that this is a time of privilege. All our principles, all our hearts, all our purposes, are being searched; searched not only by our own consciences, but searched by the world; and it is time for the people of the States of this country to show the world in

what practical sense they have learned the lessons of democracy--
that they are fighting for democracy because they believe it, and
that there is no application of democracy which they do not believe
in.

I feel, therefore, that I am standing upon the firmest foundations
of the age in bidding godspeed to the cause which you represent
and in expressing the ardent hope that the people of New York may
realize the great occasion which faces them on Election Day and
may respond to it in noble fashion.

96

XV

THE THANKSGIVING DAY PROCLAMA-TION

(November 7, 1917)

It has long been the honored custom of our people to turn in the fruitful autumn of the year in praise and thanksgiving to Almighty God for His many blessings and mercies to us as a Nation. That custom we can follow now, even in the midst of the tragedy of a world shaken by war and immeasurable disaster, in the midst of sorrow and great peril, because even amidst the darkness that has gathered about us we can see the great blessings God has bestowed upon us; blessings that are better than mere peace of mind and prosperity of enterprise.

We have been given the opportunity to serve mankind as we once served ourselves in the great day of our declaration of independence, by taking up arms against a tyranny that threatened to master and debase men everywhere and joining with other free peoples in demanding for all the nations of the world what we then demanded and obtained for ourselves. 97In this day of the revelation of our duty not only to defend our rights as a Nation, but to defend also the rights of free men throughout the world, there has been vouchsafed us in full and inspiring measure the resolution and spirit of united action. We have been brought to one mind and purpose. A new vigor of common counsel and common action has been revealed in us.

We should especially thank God that, in such circumstances, in the midst of the greatest enterprise the spirits of men have ever entered upon, we have, if we but observe a reasonable and practicable economy, abundance with which to supply the needs of those associated with us as well as our own.

A new light shines about us. The great duties of a new day awaken a new and greater national spirit in us. We shall never again be divided or wonder what stuff we are made of.

And while we render thanks for these things, let us pray Almighty God that in all humbleness of spirit we may look always to Him for guidance; that we may be kept constant in the spirit and purpose of service; that by His grace our minds may be directed and our hands strengthened, and that in His good time liberty and security and peace and the comradeship of a common justice may be vouchsafed all the nations of the earth.

Wherefore, I, Woodrow Wilson, President of 98the United States of America, do hereby designate Thursday, the 29th day of November next, as a day of thanksgiving and prayer, and invite the people throughout the land to cease upon that day from their ordinary occupations and in their several homes and places of worship to render thanks to God, the Great Ruler of nations.

99

XVI

LABOR MUST BEAR ITS PART

(November 12, 1917)

In his address before the American Federation of Labor, assembled in convention at Buffalo, New York, the President spoke as follows:

Mr. President, Delegates of the American Federation of Labor, Ladies and Gentlemen,--I esteem it a great privilege and a real honor to be thus admitted to your public councils. When your executive committee paid me the compliment of inviting me here I gladly accepted the invitation, because it seems to me that this, above all other times in your history, is the time for common counsel, for the drawing not only of the energies, but of the minds of the nation together. I thought that it was a welcome opportunity for disclosing to you some of the thoughts that have been gathering in my mind during the last momentous months.

I am introduced to you as the President of the United States, and yet I would be pleased if you would put the thought of the office into 100the background and regard me as one of your fellow-citizens who has come here to speak, not the words of authority, but the words of counsel, the words which men should speak to one another who wish to be frank in a moment more critical, perhaps, than the history of the world has ever yet known, a moment when it is every man's duty to forget himself, to forget his own interests, to fill himself with the nobility of a great national and world conception and act upon a new platform elevated above the ordinary affairs of life, elevated to where men have views of the long destiny of mankind.

I think that in order to realize just what this moment of counsel is, it is very desirable that we should remind ourselves just how this war came about and just what it is for. You can explain most wars very simply, but the explanation of this is not so simple. Its roots run deep into all the obscure soils of history, and, in my view, this is the last decisive issue between the old principles of power and the new principles of freedom.

GERMANY RESPONSIBLE FOR THE WAR

The war was started by Germany. Her authorities deny that they started it, but I am willing to let the statement I have just made await the verdict of history. The thing that needs to be explained is why Germany started the war. Remember what the position of Germany 101in the world was--as enviable a position as any nation has ever occupied. The whole world stood at admiration of her wonderful intellectual and material achievements, and all the intellectual men of the world went to school to her. As a university man I have been surrounded by men trained in Germany, men who had resorted to Germany because nowhere else could they get such thorough and searching training, particularly in the principles of science and the principles that underlie modern material achievements.

Her men of science had made her industries perhaps the most competent industries in the world, and the label, "Made in Germany," was a guarantee of good workmanship and of sound material. She had access to all the markets of the world, and every other man who traded in those markets feared Germany because of her effective and almost irresistible competition. She had a place in the sun. Why was she not satisfied? What more did she want? There was nothing in the world of peace that she did not already have, and have in abundance.

We boast of the extraordinary pace of American advancement. We show with pride the statistics of the increase of our industries and of the population of our cities. Well, those statistics did not match the recent statistics of Germany. Her old cities took on 102youth, grew faster than any American cities ever grew; her old industries opened their eyes and saw a new world and went out for its conquest, and yet the authorities of Germany were not satisfied.

You have one part of the answer to the question why she was not satisfied in her methods of competition. There is no important industry in Germany upon which the Government had not laid its hands to direct it and, when necessity arose, control it.

You have only to ask any man whom you meet who is familiar with the conditions that prevailed before the war in the matter of international competition to find out the methods of competition which the German manufacturers and exporters used under the patronage and support of the Government of Germany. You will find that they were the same sorts of competition that we have decided to prevent by law within our own borders. If they could not sell their goods cheaper than we could sell ours, at a profit to themselves, they could get a subsidy from the Government which made it possible to sell them cheaper anyhow; and the conditions of competition were thus controlled in large measure by the German Government itself.

But that did not satisfy the German Government. All the while there was lying behind its thought, in its dreams of the future, a 103political control which would enable it, in the long run, to dominate the labor and the industry of the world.

SUCCESS BY AUTHORITY

They were not content with success by superior achievement; they wanted success by authority. I suppose very few of you have thought much about the Berlin to Bagdad railway. The Berlin to Bagdad railway was constructed in order to run the threat of force down the flank of the industrial undertakings of half a dozen other countries, so that when German competition came in it would not be resisted too far--because there was always the possibility of getting German armies into the heart of that country quicker than any other armies could be got there.

Look at the map of Europe now. Germany, in thrusting upon us again and again the discussion of peace, talks about what? Talks about Belgium, talks about northern France, talks about Alsace-Lorraine. She has kept all that her dreams contemplated when the war began. If she can keep that, her power can disturb the world as long as she keeps it; always provided--for I feel bound to put this provision in--always provided the present influences that control the German Government continue to control it.

I believe that the spirit of freedom can get 104into the hearts of Germans and find as fine a welcome there as it can find in any other hearts. But the spirit of freedom does not suit the plans of the Pan-Germans. Power cannot be used with concentrated force against free peoples if it is used by free people. You know how many intimations come to us from one of the Central Powers that it is more anxious for peace than the chief Central Power, and you know that it means that the people in that Central Power know that if the war ends as it stands, they will in effect themselves be vassals of Germany, notwithstanding that their populations are compounded with all the people of that part of the world, and notwithstanding the fact that they do not wish, in their pride and proper spirit of nationality, to be so absorbed and dominated.

THE POLITICAL POWER OF THE WORLD

Germany is determined that the political power of the world shall belong to her. There have been such ambitions before. They have been in part realized. But never before have those ambitions been based upon so exact and precise and scientific a plan of domination.

May I not say it is amazing to me that any group of people should be so ill informed as to suppose, as some groups in Russia apparently suppose, that any reforms planned in the interest of the people can live in the presence of 105a Germany powerful enough to undermine or overthrow them by intrigue or force?

Any body of free men that compounds with the present German Government is compounding for its own destruction. But that is not the whole of the story. Any man in America or anywhere else who supposes that the free industry and enterprise of the world can continue if the Pan-German plan is achieved and German power fastened upon the world is as fatuous as the dreamers of Russia.

What I am opposed to is not the feeling of the pacifists, but their stupidity. My heart is with them, but my mind has a contempt for them. I want peace, but I know how to get it, and they do not.

You will notice that I sent a friend of mine, Colonel House, to Europe, who is as great a lover of peace as any man in the world; but I did not send him on a peace mission. I sent him to take part in a conference as to how the war was to be won. And he knows, as I know, that that is the way to get peace if you want it for more than a few minutes.

If we are true friends of freedom--our own or anybody else's--we will see that the power of this country and the productivity of this country is raised to its absolute maximum and that absolutely nobody is allowed to stand in the way of it.

When I say that nobody ought to be 106allowed to stand in the way, I don't mean that they shall be prevented by the power of Government, but by the power of the American spirit. Our duty, if we are to do this great thing and show America to be what we believe her to be, the greatest hope and energy in the world, then we must stand together night and day until the job is finished.

LABOR MUST BE FREE

While we are fighting for freedom we must see, among other things, that labor is free, and that means a number of interesting things. It means not only that we must do what we have declared our purpose to do--see that the conditions of labor are not rendered more onerous by the war--but also that we shall see to it that the instrumentalities by which the conditions of labor are improved are not blocked or checked. That we must do. That has been the matter about which I have taken pleasure in conferring, from time to time, with your president, Mr. Gompers; and if I may be permitted to do so, I want to express my admiration of his patriotic courage, his large vision, his statesman-like sense and a mind that knows how to pull in harness. The horses that kick over the traces will have to be put in a corral.

Now, to "stand together" means that nobody must interrupt the processes of our energy 107if the interruption can possibly be avoided without the absolute invasion of freedom. To put it concretely, that means this: Nobody has a right to stop the processes of labor until all the methods of conciliation and settlement have been exhausted, and I might as well say right here that I am not talking to you alone. You sometimes stop the courses of labor, but there are others who do the same. I am speaking of my own experience when I say that you are reasonable in a larger number of cases than the capitalists.

I am not saying these things to them personally yet, because I haven't had a chance. But they have to be said, not in any spirit of criticism.

But, in order to clear the atmosphere and come down to business, everybody on both sides has got to transact business, and the settlement is never impossible when both sides want to do the square and right thing. Moreover, a settlement is always hard to avoid when the parties can be brought face to face. I can differ with a man much more radically when he isn't in the room than I can when he is in the room, because then the awkward thing is that he can come back at me and answer what I say. It is always dangerous for a man to have the floor entirely to himself. And, therefore, we must insist in every instance that the parties come into each other's presence and 108there discuss the issues between them, and not separately in places which have no communication with each other.

I like to remind myself of a delightful saying of an Englishman of a past generation, Charles Lamb. He was with a group of friends and he spoke harshly of some man who was not present. I ought to say that Lamb stuttered a little bit. And one of his friends said, "Why, Charles, I didn't know that you knew So-and-so?" "Oh," he said, "I don't. I can't hate a man I know."

There is a great deal of human nature, of very pleasant human nature, in that saying. It is hard to hate a man you know. I may admit, parenthetically, that there are some politicians whose methods I do not at all believe in, but they are jolly good fellows, and if they would not talk the wrong kind of politics with me I would love to be with them. And so it is all along the line, in serious matters and things less serious. We are all of the same clay and spirit, and we can get together if we desire to get together.

AMERICANS MUST CO-OPERATE

Therefore my counsel to you is this: Let us show ourselves Americans by showing that we do not want to go off in separate camps or groups by ourselves, but that we want to co-operate with all other classes and all other 109groups in a common enterprise, which is to release the spirits of the world from bondage. I would be willing to set that up as the final test of an American. That is the meaning of democracy.

I have been very much distressed, my fellow-citizens, by some of the things that have happened recently. The mob spirit is displaying itself here and there in this country. I have no sympathy with what some men are saying, but I have no sympathy with the men that take their punishment into their own hands; and I want to say to every man who does join such a mob that I recognize him as unworthy of the free institutions of the United States.

There are some organizations in this country whose object is anarchy and the destruction of the law. I despise and hate their purpose as much as any man, but I respect the ancient processes of justice, and I would be too proud not to see them done justice, however wrong they are. And so I want to utter my earnest protest against any manifestation of the spirit of lawlessness anywhere or in any cause. Why, gentlemen, look what it means.

We claim to be the greatest democratic people in the world, and democracy means, first of all, that we can govern ourselves. If our men have not self-control, then they are not capable of that great thing which we call 110democratic government. A man who takes the law into his own hands is not the right man to co-operate in any form of orderly development of law and institutions.

And some of the processes by which the struggle between capital and labor is carried on are processes that come very near to taking the law into your own hands. I do not mean for a moment to compare them with what I have just been speaking of, but I want you to see that they are mere gradations of the manifestations of the unwillingness to co-operate. The fundamental lesson of the whole situation is that we must not only take common counsel, but that we must yield to and obey common counsel. Not all of the instrumentalities for this are at hand.

BETTER CONDITIONS MAY BE AT HAND

111

I am hopeful that in the very near future new instrumentalities may be organized by which we can see to it that various things that are now going on shall not go on. There are various processes of the dilution of labor and the unnecessary substitution of labor and bidding in different markets and unfairly upsetting the whole competition of labor which ought not to go on--I mean now, on the part of employers--and we must interject into this some instrumentality of co-operation by which the fair thing will be done all around.

I am hopeful that some such instrumentalities may be devised, but whether they are or not we must use those that we have, and upon every occasion where it is necessary to have such an instrumentality, originated upon that occasion, if necessary.

And so, my fellow-citizens, the reason that I came away from Washington is that I sometimes get lonely down there--there are so many people in Washington who know things that are not so, and there are so few people in Washington who know anything about what the people of the United States are thinking about. I have to come away to get reminded of the rest of the country. I have come away and talk to men who are up against the real thing and say to them, I am with you if you are with me. The only test of being with me is not to think about me personally at all, but merely to think of me as the expression for the time being of the power and dignity and hope of the American people.

XVII

ADDRESS TO CONGRESS

(December 4, 1917)

Gentlemen of the Congress,--Eight months have elapsed since I last had the honor of addressing you. They have been months crowded with events of immense and grave significance for us. I shall not undertake to detail or even to summarize these events. The practical particulars of the part we have played in them will be laid before you in the reports of the executive departments. I shall discuss only our present outlook upon these vast affairs, our present duties and the immediate means of accomplishing the objects we shall hold always in view.

I shall not go back to debate the causes of the war. The intolerable wrongs done and planned against us by the sinister masters of Germany have long since become too grossly obvious and odious to every true American to need to be rehearsed. But I shall ask you to consider again, and with very grave scrutiny, 113our objectives and the measures by which we mean to attain them; for the purpose of discussion here in this place is action, and our action must move straight toward definite ends. Our object is, of course, to win the war, and we shall not slacken or suffer ourselves to be diverted until it is won. But it is worth while asking and answering the question, When shall we consider the war won?

From one point of view it is not necessary to broach this fundamental matter. I do not doubt that the American people know what the war is about, and what sort of an outcome they will regard as a realization of their purpose in it. As a nation we are united in spirit and intention.

I pay little heed to those who tell me otherwise. I hear the voices of dissent--who does not? I hear the criticism and the clamor of the noisily thoughtless and troublesome. I also see men here and there fling themselves in impotent disloyalty against the calm, indomitable power of the Nation. I hear men debate peace who understand

neither its nature nor the way in which we may attain it, with up-
lifted eyes and unbroken spirits. But I know that none of these
speaks for the Nation. They do not touch the heart of anything.
They may safely be left to strut about their uneasy hour and be forgotten.

114

WHAT WE ARE FIGHTING FOR

But from another point of view I believe that it is necessary to say
plainly what we here at the seat of action consider the war to be for,
and what part we mean to play in the settlement of its searching
issues. We are the spokesmen of the American people, and they
have a right to know whether their purpose is ours. They desire
peace by the overcoming of evil, but the defeat once and for all of
the sinister forces that interrupt peace and render it impossible, and
they wish to know how closely our thought runs with theirs and
what action we propose. They are impatient with those who desire
peace by any sort of compromise--deeply and indignantly impa-
tient--but they will be equally impatient with us if we do not make
it plain to them what our objectives are and what we are planning
for in seeking to make conquest of peace by arms.

I believe that I speak for them when I say two things: First, that
this intolerable Thing of which the masters of Germany have shown
us the ugly face, this menace of combined intrigue and force, which
we now see so clearly as the German power, a Thing without conscience or honor or capacity for covenanted peace, must be crushed,
and, if it be not utterly brought to an end, at least shut out from the
friendly intercourse of the nations; and, second, that when 115this
Thing and its power are indeed defeated and the time comes that
we can discuss peace--when the German people have spokesmen
whose word we can believe, and when those spokesmen are ready,
in the name of their people, to accept the common judgment of the
nations as to what shall henceforth be the bases of law and of covenant for the life of the world--we shall be willing and glad to pay
the full price for peace and pay it ungrudgingly. We know what
that price will be. It will be full, impartial justice--justice done at

every point and to every nation that the final settlement must affect, our enemies as well as our friends.

You catch with me the voices of humanity that are in the air. They grow daily more audible, more articulate, more persuasive, and they come from the hearts of 116men everywhere. They insist that the war shall not end in vindictive action of any kind; that no nation or people shall be robbed or punished because the irresponsible rulers of a single country have themselves done deep and abominable wrong. It is this thought that has been expressed in the formula, "No annexations, no contributions, no punitive indemnities."

THE PEOPLE OF RUSSIA LED ASTRAY

Just because this crude formula expresses the instinctive judgment as to the right of plain men everywhere, it has been made diligent use of by the masters of German intrigue to lead the people of Russia astray, and the people of every other country their agents could reach, in order that a premature peace might be brought about before autocracy has been taught its final and convincing lesson and the people of the world put in control of their own destinies.

But the fact that a wrong use has been made of a just idea is no reason why a right use should not be made of it. It ought to be brought under the patronage of its real friends. Let it be said again that autocracy must first be shown the utter futility of its claims to power or leadership in the modern world. It is impossible to apply any standard of justice so long as such forces are unchecked and undefeated as the present masters of Germany command. Not until that has been done can right be set up as arbiter and peacemaker among the nations. But when that has been done--as, God willing, it assuredly will be--we shall at last be free to do an unprecedented thing, and this is the time to avow our purpose to do it. We shall be free to base peace on generosity and justice, to the exclusion of all selfish claims to advantage, even on the part of the victors.

Let there be no misunderstanding. Our present and immediate task is to win the war, 117and nothing shall turn us aside from it until it is accomplished. Every power and resource we possess, whether of men, of money, or of materials, is being devoted, and will continue to be devoted, to that purpose until it is achieved. Those who desire to bring peace about before that purpose is achieved I counsel to carry their advice elsewhere. We will not entertain it.

JUSTICE AND REPARATION

We shall regard the war only as won when the German people say to us, through properly accredited representatives, that they are ready to agree to a settlement based upon justice and the reparation of the wrongs their rulers have done. They have done a wrong to Belgium which must be repaired. They have established a power over other lands and peoples than their own--over the great empire of Austria-Hungary, over hitherto free Balkan states, over Turkey, and within Asia--which must be relinquished.

Germany's success by skill, by industry, by knowledge, by enterprise, we did not grudge or oppose, but admired rather. She had built up for herself a real empire of trade and influence, secured by the peace of the world. We were content to abide the rivalries of manufacture, science and commerce that were involved for us in her success, and stand or fall as we had 118or did not have the brains and the initiative to surpass her. But at the moment when she had conspicuously won her triumphs of peace she threw them away to establish in their stead what the world will no longer permit to be established--military and political domination by arms, by which to oust where she could not excel the rivals she most feared and hated.

The peace we make must remedy that wrong. It must deliver the once fair lands and happy peoples of Belgium and northern France from the Prussian conquest and the Prussian menace, but it must also deliver the peoples of Austria-Hungary, the peoples of the Balkans, and the peoples of Turkey, alike in Europe and in Asia, from the impudent and alien domination of the Prussian military and commercial autocracy.

We owe it, however, to ourselves to say that we do not wish in any way to impair or to rearrange the Austro-Hungarian Empire. It is no affair of ours what they do with their own life, either industrially or politically. We do not purpose nor desire to dictate to them in any way. We only desire to see that their affairs are left in their own hands, in all matters, great or small. We shall hope to secure for the peoples of the Balkan peninsula and for the people of the Turkish Empire the right and opportunity to make their own lives safe, their 119own fortunes secure against oppression or injustice and from the dictation of foreign courts or parties, and our attitude and purpose with regard to Germany herself are of a like kind.

OUR ATTITUDE TOWARD GERMANY

We intend no wrong against the German Empire, no interference with her internal affairs. We should deem either the one or the other absolutely unjustifiable, absolutely contrary to the principles we have professed to live by and to hold most sacred throughout our life as a nation.

The people of Germany are being told by the men whom they now permit to deceive them and to act as their masters that they are fighting for very life and existence of their empire, a war of desperate self-defense against deliberate aggression. Nothing could be more grossly or wantonly false, and we must seek, by the utmost openness and candor as to our real aims, to convince them of its falseness. We are, in fact, fighting for their emancipation from fear, along with our own, from the fear as well as from the fact of unjust attack by neighbors or rivals or schemers after world empire. No one is threatening the existence or the independence or the peaceful enterprise of the German Empire.

The worst that can happen to the detriment of the German people is this, that if they should 120still, after the war is over, continue to be obliged to live under ambitious and intriguing masters interested to disturb the peace of the world, men or classes of men whom the other peoples of the world could not trust, it might be impossible to admit them to the partnership of nations which must henceforth guarantee the world's peace. That partnership must be a partnership of peoples, not a mere partnership of governments.

It might be impossible, also, in such untoward circumstances, to admit Germany to the free economic intercourse which must inevitably spring out of the other partnerships of a real peace. But there would be no aggression in that; and such a situation, inevitable because of distrust, would in the very nature of things sooner or later cure itself, by processes which would assuredly set in.

THE RIGHTS OF THE CENTRAL POWERS

The wrongs, the very deep wrongs, committed in this war will have to be righted. That of course. But they cannot and must not be righted by the commission of similar wrongs against Germany and her allies. The world will not permit the commission of similar wrongs as a means of reparation and settlement. Statesmen must by this time have learned that the opinion of the world is everywhere wide awake and fully comprehends the 121issues involved. No representative of any self-governed nation will dare disregard it by attempting any such covenants of selfishness and compromise as were entered into at the congress of Vienna.

The thought of the plain people here and everywhere throughout the world, the people who enjoy no privilege and have very simple and unsophisticated standards of right and wrong, is the air all governments must henceforth breathe if they would live. It is in the full disclosing light of that thought that all policies must be conceived and executed in this midday hour of the world's life.

German rulers have been able to upset the peace of the world only because the German people were not suffered, under their tutelage, to share the comradeship of the other peoples of the world either in thought or in purpose. They were allowed to have no opinion of their own which might be set up as a rule of conduct for those who exercised authority over them. But the congress that concludes this war will feel the full strength of the tides that run now in the hearts and consciences of free men everywhere. Its conclusions will run with those tides.

All these things have been true from the very beginning of this stupendous war; and I cannot help thinking that if they had been made plain at the very outset the sympathy and 122enthusiasm of the Russian people might have been once for all enlisted on the side of the Allies, suspicion and distrust swept away, and a real and lasting union of purpose effected. Had they believed these things at the very moment of their revolution, and had they been confirmed in that belief since, the sad reverses which have recently marked the progress of their affairs toward an ordered and stable government of free men might have been avoided.

TRUTH AS THE ANTIDOTE

The Russian people have been poisoned by the very same falsehoods that have kept the German people in the dark, and the poison has been administered by the very same hands. The only possible antidote is the truth. It cannot be uttered too plainly or too often.

From every point of view, therefore, it has seemed to be my duty to speak these declarations of purpose, to add these specific interpretations to what I took the liberty of saying to the Senate in January. Our entrance into the war has not altered our attitude toward the settlement that must come when it is over. When I said in January that the nations of the world were entitled not only to free pathways upon the sea, but also to assured and unmolested access to those pathways, I was thinking, and I am thinking now, not of the smaller and weaker nations alone, which need 123our countenance and support, but also of the great and powerful nations, and of our present enemies as well as our present associates in the war. I was thinking, and am thinking now, of Austria herself, among the rest, as well as of Serbia and of Poland. Justice and equality of rights can be had only at a great price. We are seeking permanent, not temporary, foundations for the peace of the world, and must seek them candidly and fearlessly. As always, the right will prove to be the expedient.

What shall we do, then, to push this great war of freedom and justice to its righteous conclusion? We must clear away with a thorough hand all impediments to success, and we must make every adjustment of law that will facilitate the full and free use of our whole capacity and force as a fighting unit.

THE WAR AGAINST AUSTRIA

One very embarrassing obstacle that stands in our way is that we are at war with Germany, but not with her allies. I therefore very earnestly recommend that the Congress immediately declare the United States in a state of war with Austria-Hungary. Does it seem strange to you that this should be the conclusion of the argument I have just addressed to you? It is not. It is, in fact, the inevitable logic of what I have said. Austria-Hungary is for the time being not her own mistress, but 124simply the vassal of the German Government. We must face the facts as they are and act upon them without sentiment in this stern business.

The Government of Austria-Hungary is not acting upon its own initiative or in response to the wishes and feelings of its own peoples, but as the instrument of another nation. We must meet its force with our own and regard the Central Powers as but one. The war can be successfully conducted in no other way. The same logic would lead also to a declaration of war against Turkey and Bulgaria. They also are the tools of Germany. But they are mere tools, and do not yet stand in the direct path of our necessary action. We shall go wherever the necessities of this war carry us, but it seems to me that we should go only where immediate and practical considerations lead us, and not heed any others.

A STRICTER GRIP ON ENEMY ALIENS

The financial and military measures which must be adopted will suggest themselves as the war and its undertakings develop, but I will take the liberty of proposing to you certain other acts of legislation which seem to me to be needed for the support of the war and for the release of our whole force and energy.

It will be necessary to extend in certain particulars the legislation of the last session with 125regard to alien enemies; and also necessary, I believe, to create a very definite and particular control over the entrance and departure of all persons into and from the United States.

Legislation should be enacted defining as a criminal offense every wilful violation of the Presidential proclamations relating to enemy aliens promulgated under Section 4067 of the Revised Statutes and providing appropriate punishment; and women as well as men should be included under the terms of the acts placing restraints upon alien enemies. It is likely that as time goes on many alien enemies will be willing to be fed and housed at the expense of the Government in the detention camps, and it would be the purpose of the legislation I have suggested to confine offenders among them in penitentiaries and other similar institutions, where they could be made to work as other criminals do.

A FURTHER LIMITING OF PRICES

Recent experience has convinced me that the Congress must go further in authorizing the Government to set limits to prices. The law of supply and demand, I am sorry to say, has been replaced by the law of unrestrained selfishness. While we have eliminated profiteering in several branches of industry, it still runs impudently rampant in others. The farmers, for example, complain with a great deal 126of justice that, while the regulation of food prices restricts their incomes, no restraints are placed upon the prices of most of the things they must themselves purchase; and similar inequities obtain on all sides.

It is imperatively necessary that the consideration of the full use of the water power of the country, and also the consideration of the systematic and yet economical development of such of the natural resources of the country as are still under the control of the Federal

Government, should be resumed and affirmatively and constructively dealt with at the earliest possible moment. The pressing need of such legislation is daily becoming more obvious.

The legislation proposed at the last session with regard to regulated combinations among our exporters, in order to provide for our foreign trade a more effective organization and method of co-operation, ought by all means to be completed at this session.

And I beg that the members of the House of Representatives will permit me to express the opinion that it will be impossible to deal in any way but a very wasteful and extravagant fashion with the enormous 127appropriations of the public moneys which must continue to be made, if the war is to be properly sustained, unless the House will consent to return to its former practice of initiating and preparing all appropriation bills through a single committee, in order that responsibility may be centered, expenditures standardized and made uniform, and waste and duplication as much as possible avoided.

Additional legislation may also become necessary before the present Congress adjourns, in order to effect the most efficient co-ordination and operation of the railway and other transportation systems of the country; but to that I shall, if circumstances should demand, call the attention of Congress upon another occasion.

THE WINNING OF THE WAR

If I have overlooked anything that ought to be done for the more effective conduct of the war, your own counsels will supply the omission. What I am perfectly clear about is that, in the present session of the Congress, our whole attention and energy should be concentrated on the vigorous and rapid and successful prosecution of the great task of winning the war.

We can do this with all the greater zeal and enthusiasm because we know that for us this is a war of high principle, debased by no selfish ambition of conquest or spoliation; because we know, and all the world knows, that we have been forced into it to save the very institutions we live under from corruption and destruction. The purposes of the Central Powers strike 128straight at the very heart of everything we believe in; their methods of warfare outrage every principle of humanity and of knightly honor; their intrigue has corrupted the very thought and spirit of many of our people; their sinister and secret diplomacy has sought to take our very territory away from us and disrupt the union of the States. Our safety would be at an end, our honor forever sullied and brought into contempt, were we to permit their triumph. They are striking at the very existence of democracy and liberty.

It is because it is for us a war of high, disinterested purpose, in which all the free people of the world are banded together for the vindication of right, a war for the preservation of our nation and of all that it has held dear of principle and of purpose, that we feel ourselves doubly constrained to propose for its outcome only that which is righteous and of irreproachable intention, for our foes as well as for our friends.

The cause being just and holy, the settlement must be of like motive and quality. For this we can fight, but for nothing less noble or less worthy of our traditions. For this cause we entered the war, and for this cause we will battle until the last gun is fired.

I have spoken plainly because this seems to me the time when it is most necessary to speak plainly, in order that all the world may know 129that even in the heat and ardor of the struggle, and when our whole thought is of carrying the war through to its end, we have not forgotten any ideal or principle for which the name of America has been held in honor among the nations and for which it has been our glory to contend in the great generations that went before us.

A supreme moment of history has come. The eyes of the people have been opened and they see. The hand of God is laid upon the nations. He will show them favor, I devoutly believe, only if they rise to the clear heights of His own justice and mercy.

130

XVIII

PROCLAMATION OF WAR AGAINST AUSTRIA-HUNGARY

(December 12, 1917)

The President's proclamation, after citing the resolution of Congress authorizing the war with Austria, says:

Now, therefore, I, Woodrow Wilson, President of the United States of America, do hereby proclaim to all whom it may concern that a state of war exists between the United States and the Imperial and Royal Austro-Hungarian Government, and I do specially direct all officers, civil or military, of the United States that they exercise vigilance and zeal in the discharge of the duties incident to such a state of war.

And I do, moreover, earnestly appeal to all American citizens that they, in loyal devotion to their country, dedicated from its foundation to the principles of liberty and justice, uphold the laws of the land and give undivided and willing support to those measures which may be adopted by the constitutional authorities 131in prosecuting the war to a successful issue and obtaining a secure and just peace.

NEED ONLY OBEY THE LAWS

And, acting under and by virtue of the authority vested in me by the Constitution of the United States, and the aforesaid sections of the Revised Statutes, I do hereby further proclaim and direct that the conduct to be observed on the part of the United States toward all natives, citizens, denizens or subjects of Austria-Hungary, being males of the age of fourteen years and upward, who shall be within the United States and not actually naturalized, shall be as follows:

> All natives, citizens, denizens or subjects of Austria-Hungary, being males of fourteen years and upward who shall be within the United States and not actually naturalized, are enjoined to preserve the peace toward the United States and to refrain from crime against the public safety and from violating the laws of the United States and of the States and Territories thereof.
>
> And to refrain from actual hostility or giving information, aid or comfort to the enemies of the United States.
>
> And to comply strictly with the regulations which are hereby or which may be, from time to time, promulgated by the President.
>
> And so long as they shall conduct themselves in accordance with law, they shall be undisturbed in the peaceful pursuit of their lives and occupations and be accorded the consideration due to all peaceful and law-abiding persons, except so far as restrictions may be 132necessary for their own protection and for the safety of the United States.

A FRIENDLY ATTITUDE IS URGED

And toward such of said persons as conduct themselves in accordance with law, all citizens of 133the United States are enjoined to preserve the peace and to treat them with all such friendliness as may be compatible with loyalty and allegiance to the United States.

And all natives, citizens, denizens or subjects of Austria-Hungary, being males of the age of fourteen years and upward, who shall be within the United States and not actually naturalized, who fail to conduct themselves as so enjoined, in addition to all other penalties prescribed by law, shall be liable to restraint or to

116

give security, or to remove and depart from the United States in the manner prescribed by Sections 4069 and 4070 of the Revised Stat utes and as prescribed in regulations duly promulgated by the President:

FEW REGULATIONS

And pursuant to the authority vested in me, I hereby declare and establish the following regulations, which I find necessary in the premises, and for the public safety:

> 1. No native, citizen, denizen or subject of Austria-Hungary, being a male of the age of fourteen years and upward and not actually naturalized, shall depart from the United States until he shall have received such permit as the President shall prescribe, or except under order of a court, judge or justice, under Sections 4069 and 4070 of the Revised Statutes.

> 2. No such person shall land or enter the United States except under such restrictions and at such places as the President may prescribe.

> 3. Every such person, of whom there may be reasonable cause to believe that he is aiding or about to aid the enemy, or who may be at large to the danger of the public peace or safety, or who violates or attempts to violate, or of whom there is reasonable ground to believe that he is about to violate any regulation duly promulgated by the President, or any criminal law of the United States, or of the States or Territories thereof, will be subject to summary arrest by the United States Marshal or his deputy, or such other officers as the President shall designate, and to confinement in such penitentiary, prison, jail, military camp or

other place of detention as may be directed by the
President.

This proclamation and the regulations herein contained shall extend and apply to all land and water, continental or insular, in any
way within the jurisdiction of the United States.

134

XIX

THE GOVERNMENT TAKES OVER THE RAILROADS

(A Statement by the President, December 26, 1917)

I have exercised the powers over the transportation systems of the country which were granted me by the Act of Congress of August, 1916, because it has become imperatively necessary for me to do so.

This is a war of resources no less than of men, perhaps even more than of men, and it is necessary for the complete mobilization of our resources that the transportation systems of the country should be organized and employed under a single authority and a simplified method of co-ordination which have not proved possible under private management and control.

The committee of railway executives who have been co-operating with the Government in this all-important matter have done the utmost that it was possible for them to do; have done it with patriotic zeal and with great ability; 135but there were differences that they could neither escape nor neutralize.

IN FAIRNESS TO THE RAILROADS

Complete unity of administration in the present circumstances involves upon occasion and at many points a serious dislocation of earnings, and the committee was, of course, without power or authority to rearrange changes or effect proper compensations and adjustments of earnings. Several roads which were willingly and with admirable public spirit accepting the orders of the committee have already suffered from these circumstances and should not be required to suffer further. In mere fairness to them the full authority of the Government must be substituted.

The Government itself will thereby gain an immense increase of efficiency in the conduct of the war and of the innumerable activities upon which its successful conduct depends.

The public interest must be first served, and in addition the financial interests of the Government and the financial interests of the railways must be brought under a common direction. The financial operations of the railways need not then interfere with the borrowings of the Government, and they themselves can be conducted at a great advantage.

136

INVESTORS TO BE PROTECTED

Investors in railway securities may rest assured that their rights and interests will be as scrupulously looked after by the Government as they could be by the directors of the several railway systems. Immediately upon the reassembling of Congress I shall recommend that these definite guarantees be given:

First, of course, that the railway properties will be maintained during the period of Federal control in as good repair and as complete equipment as when taken over by the Government, and, second, that the roads shall receive a net operating income equal in each case to the average net income of the three years preceding June 30, 1917; and I am entirely confident that the Congress will be disposed in this case, as in others, to see that justice is done and full security assured to the owners and creditors of the great systems which the Government must now use under its own direction or else suffer serious embarrassment.

The Secretary of War and I are agreed that, all the circumstances being taken into consideration, the best results can be obtained under the immediate executive direction of the Hon. William G. McAdoo, whose practical experience peculiarly fits him for the service, and whose authority as Secretary of the Treasury will enable him to co-ordinate, as no other man 137could, the many financial interests which will be involved and which might, unless systematically directed, suffer very embarrassing entanglements.

A RECOGNITION OF FACTS

The Government of the United States is the only great Government now engaged in the war which has not already assumed control of this sort. It was thought to be in the spirit of American institutions to attempt to do everything that was necessary through private management, and if zeal and ability and patriotic motive could have accomplished the necessary unification of administration, it would certainly have been accomplished; but no zeal or ability could overcome insuperable obstacles and I have deemed it my duty to recognize that fact in all candor, now that it is demonstrated, and to use without reserve the great authority reposed in me.

A great national necessity dictated the action, and I was therefore not at liberty to abstain from it.

Woodrow Wilson.

The text of the proclamation follows:

Whereas, the Congress of the United States, in the exercise of the constitutional authority vested in them, by joint resolution of the Senate and House of Representatives, bearing date April 6, 1917, resolved:

138

"That the state of war between the United States and the Imperial German Government which has thus been thrust upon the United States is hereby formally declared, and that the President be, and he is hereby, authorized and directed to employ the entire naval and military forces of the United States and the resources of the Government to carry on war against the Imperial German Government, and to bring the conflict to a successful termination, all of the resources of the country are hereby pledged by the Congress of the United States."

And by joint resolution bearing date of December 7, 1917, resolved:

> "That a state of war is hereby declared to exist between the United States of America and the Imperial and Royal Austro-Hungarian Government, and that the President be, and he is hereby, authorized and directed to employ the entire naval and military forces of the United States and the resources of the Government to carry on war against the Imperial and Royal Austro-Hungarian Government, and to bring the conflict to a successful termination, all the resources of the country are hereby pledged by the Congress of the United States."

And whereas, it is provided by Section 1 of the act approved August 29, 1916, entitled "An act making appropriations for the support of the army for the fiscal year ending June 30, 1917, and for other purposes," as follows:

"The President, in time of war, is empowered, through the Secretary of War, to take possession and assume control of any system or systems of transportation, or any part thereof, and to utilize the same, to the exclusion as far as may be necessary of all other traffic thereon, for the transfer or transportation of troops, war material and equipment, or for such other 139purposes connected with the emergency as may be needful or desirable."

And whereas, it has now become necessary in the national defense to take possession and assume control of certain systems of transportation and to utilize the same, to the exclusion as far as may be necessary of other than war traffic thereon for the transportation of troops, war material and equipment therefor, and for other needful and desirable purposes connected with the prosecution of the war.

Now, therefore, I, Woodrow Wilson, President of the United States, under and by virtue of the powers vested in me by the foregoing resolutions and statute, and by virtue of all other powers thereto me enabling, do hereby, through Newton D. Baker, Secretary of War, take possession and assume control at 12 o'clock noon on the twenty-eighth day of December, 1917, of each and every system of transportation and the appurtenances thereof located wholly or in part within the boundaries of the continental United States and consisting of railroads, and owned or controlled systems of coastwise and inland transportation, engaged in general transportation, whether operated by steam or by electric power, including also terminals, terminal companies and terminal associations, sleeping and parlor cars, private cars and private car lines, elevators, warehouses, telegraph and telephone lines and all other equipment and appurtenances commonly used upon or operated as a part of such rail or combined rail and water systems of transportation, to the end that such systems of transportation be utilized for the transfer and transportation of troops, war material and equipment to the exclusion so far as may be necessary of all other traffic thereon, and that so far as such exclusive use be not necessary or desirable, such systems of transportation be operated and utilized in the performance of such other services as the national interest 140may require and of the usual and ordinary business and duties of common carriers.

It is hereby directed that the possession, control, operation and utilization of such transportation systems hereby by me undertaken shall be exercised by and through William G. McAdoo, who is hereby appointed and designated Director-General of Railroads.

Said director may perform the duties imposed upon him, so long and to such extent as he shall determine, through the boards of directors, receivers, officers and employees of said systems of transportation. Until and except so far as said director shall from time to time by general or special orders otherwise provide, the boards of directors, receivers, officers and employees of the various transportation systems shall continue the operation thereof in the usual and ordinary course of the business of common carriers, in the names of their respective companies.

Until and except so far as said director shall from time to time otherwise by general or special orders determine, such systems of transportation shall remain subject to all existing statutes and orders of the Interstate Commerce Commission, and to all statutes and orders of regulating commissions of the various States in which said systems or any part thereof may be situated. But any orders, general or special, hereafter made by said director shall have paramount authority and be obeyed as such.

Nothing herein shall be construed as now affecting the possession, operation and control of street electric passenger railways, including railways commonly called interurban, whether such railways be or be not owned or controlled by such railroad companies or systems. By subsequent order and proclamation, if and when it shall be found necessary or desirable, possession, control or operation may be taken of all or any part of such street railway systems, including subways and tunnels, and by subsequent order and proclamation possession, control 141and operation in whole or in part may also be relinquished to the owners thereof of any part of the railroad systems or rail and water systems, possession and control of which are hereby assumed.

The director shall as soon as may be after having assumed such possession and control enter upon negotiations with the several companies looking to agreements for just and reasonable compensation for the possession, use and control of the respective properties on the basis of an annual guaranteed compensation, above accruing depreciation and the maintenance of their properties, equivalent, as nearly as may be, to the average of the net operating income thereof for the three year period ending June 30, 1917--the results of such negotiations to be reported to me for such action as may be appropriate and lawful.

But nothing herein contained, expressed or implied, or hereafter done or suffered hereunder, shall be deemed in any way to impair the rights of the stockholders, bondholders, creditors and other persons having interests in said systems of transportation or in the profits thereof, to receive just and adequate compensation for the use and control and operation of their property hereby assumed.

Regular dividends hitherto declared, and maturing interest upon bonds, debentures and other obligations, may be paid in due course, and such regular dividends and interest may continue to be paid until and unless the said director shall from time to time otherwise by general or special orders determine, and, subject to the approval of the director, the various carriers may agree upon and arrange for the renewal and extension of maturing obligations.

Except with the prior written assent of said director, no attachment by mesne process or on execution shall be levied on or against any of the property used by any of said transportation systems, in the conduct of their 142business as common carriers; but suits may be brought by and against said carriers and judgments rendered as hitherto until and except so far as said director may, by general or special orders, otherwise determine.

From and after 12 o'clock on said twenty-eighth day of December, 1917, all transportation systems included in this order and proclamation shall conclusively be deemed within the possession and control of said director without further act or notice, but for the purpose of accounting said possession and control shall date from 12 o'clock midnight on December 31, 1917.

In witness whereof, I have hereunto set my hand and caused the seal of the United States to be affixed.

Done by the President, through Newton D. Baker, Secretary of War, in the District of Columbia, this twenty-sixth day of December, in the year of our Lord one thousand nine hundred and seventeen, and of Independence of the United States the one hundred and forty-second.

Woodrow Wilson.

Newton D. Baker, Secretary of War.

By the President:

Robert Lansing, Secretary of State.

143

XX

GOVERNMENT OPERATION OF RAILROADS

(Address to the Congress, January 4, 1918)

Gentlemen of the Congress,--I have asked the privilege of addressing you in order to report that on the 28th of December last, during the recess of Congress, acting through the Secretary of War, and under the authority conferred upon me by the Act of Congress approved August 29, 1916, I took possession and assumed control of the railway lines of the country and the systems of water transportation under their control. This step seemed to be imperatively necessary in the interest of the public welfare, in the presence of the great tasks of war with which we are now dealing. As our experience develops difficulties and makes it clear what they are, I have deemed it my duty to remove those difficulties wherever I have the legal power to do so.

To assume control of the vast railway systems of the country is, I realize, a very great responsibility, but to fail to do so in the existing circumstances would have been much greater. 144I assumed the less responsibility rather than the weightier.

NEED OF UNITED DIRECTION

I am sure that I am speaking the mind of all thoughtful Americans when I say that it is our duty as the representatives of the nation to do everything that it is necessary to do to secure the complete mobilization of the whole resources of America by as rapid and effective a means as can be found. Transportation supplies all the arteries of mobilization. Unless it be under a single and unified direction, the whole process of the nation's action is embarrassed.

It was in the true spirit of America, and it was right, that we should first try to effect the necessary unification under the voluntary action of those who were in charge of the great railway properties, and we did try it. The directors of the railways responded to the need promptly and generously. The group of railway executives who were charged with the task of actual co-ordination and general direction performed their difficult duties with patriotic zeal and marked ability, as was to have been expected, and did, I believe, everything that it was possible for them to do in the circumstances. If I have taken the task out of their hands, it has not been because of any dereliction or failure on their part, but only 145because there were some things which the Government can do, and private management cannot. We shall continue to value most highly the advice and assistance of these gentlemen, and I am sure we shall not find them withholding it.

It had become unmistakably plain that only under Government administration can the entire equipment of the several systems of transportation be fully and unreservedly thrown into a common service without injurious discrimination against particular properties; only under Government administration can absolutely unrestricted and unembarrassed common use be made of all tracks, terminal facilities and equipment of every kind. Only under that authority can new terminals be constructed and developed without regard to the requirements or limitations of particular roads. But under Government administration all these things will be possible--not instantly, but as fast as practical difficulties, which cannot be merely conjured away, give way before the new management.

AS LITTLE DISTURBANCE AS POSSIBLE

The common administration will be carried out with as little disturbance of the present operating organizations and personnel of the railways as possible. Nothing will be altered or disturbed which is not necessary to disturb. 146We are serving the public interest and safeguarding the public safety, but we are also regardful of the interest of those by whom these great properties are owned and glad to avail ourselves of the experience and trained ability of those who have been managing them. It is necessary that the transportation of troops and of war materials, of food and of fuel, and of everything that is necessary for the full mobilization of the energies and resources of the country, should be first considered; but it is clearly in the public interest also that the ordinary activities and the normal industrial and commercial life of the country should be interfered with and dislocated as little as possible, and the public may rest assured that the interest and convenience of the private shipper will be carefully served and safeguarded as it is possible to serve and safeguard it in the present extraordinary circumstances.

COMPENSATION SHOULD BE GUARANTEED

While the present authority of the Executive suffices for all purposes of administration, and while, of course, all private interests must for the present give way to the public necessity, it is, I am sure you will agree with me, right and necessary that the owners and creditors of the railways, the holders of their stocks and bonds, should receive from the Government an unqualified guarantee that their properties 147will be maintained throughout the period of Federal control in as good repair and as complete equipment as at present, and that the several roads will receive, under Federal management, such compensation as is equitable and just alike to their owners and to the general public. I would suggest the average net railway operating income of the three years ending June 30, 1917. I earnestly recommend that these guarantees be given by appropriate legislation, and given as promptly as circumstances permit.

I need not point out the essential justice of such guarantees and their great influence and significance as elements in the present financial and industrial situation of the country. Indeed, one of the strong arguments for assuming control of the railroads at this time is the financial argument. It is necessary that the values of railway securities should be justly and fairly protected, and that the largest financial operations every year necessary in connection with the maintenance, operation and development of the roads should, during the period of the war, be wisely related to the financial operations of the Government.

Our first duty is, of course, to conserve the common interest and the common safety, and to make certain that nothing stands in the way of the successful prosecution of the great war for liberty and justice; but it is an obligation 148of public conscience and of public honor that the private interests we disturb should be kept safe from unjust injury, and it is of the utmost consequence to the Government itself that all great financial operations should be stabilized and co-ordinated with the financial operations of the Government. No borrowing should run athwart the borrowings of the Federal Treasury, and no fundamental industrial values should anywhere be unnecessarily impaired. In the hands of many thousands of small investors in the country, as well as in national banks, in insurance companies, in savings banks, in trust companies, in financial agencies of every kind, railway securities--the sum total of which runs up to some ten or eleven thousand millions, constitute a vital part of the structure of credit, and the unquestioned solidity of that structure must be maintained.

SELECTION OF MCADOO AS DIRECTOR

The Secretary of War and I easily agreed that, in view of the many complex interests which must be safeguarded and harmonized, as well as because of his exceptional experience and ability in this new field of governmental action, the Hon. William G. McAdoo was the right man to assume direct administrative control of this new executive task. At our request, he consented to assume the authority and duties of organizer and director-general of 149the new railway administration. He has assumed those duties, and his work is in active progress.

It is probably too much to expect that, even under the unified railway administration which will now be possible, sufficient economies can be effected in the operation of the railways to make it possible to add to their equipment and extend their operative facilities as much as the present extraordinary demands upon their use will render desirable, without resorting to the national Treasury for the funds. If it is not possible, it will, of course, be necessary to resort to the Congress for grants of money for that purpose. The Secretary of the Treasury will advise with your committees with regard to this very practical aspect of the matter. For the present, I suggest only the guarantees I have indicated and such appropriations as are necessary at the outset of this task.

I take the liberty of expressing the hope that the Congress may grant these promptly and ungrudgingly. We are dealing with great matters, and will, I am sure, deal with them greatly.

150

XXI

THE TERMS OF PEACE

(January 8, 1918)

In an address to both Houses of Congress, assembled in joint session, President Wilson enunciated the war and peace 151program of the United States in fourteen definite proposals. The President spoke as follows:

Gentlemen of the Congress,--Once more, as repeatedly before, the spokesmen of the Central Empires have indicated their desires to discuss the objects of the war and the possible basis of a general peace. Parleys have been in progress at Brest-Litovsk between Russian representatives and representatives of the Central Powers to which the attention of all the belligerents has been invited for the purpose of ascertaining whether it may be possible to extend these parleys into a general conference with regard to terms of peace and settlement.

The Russian representatives presented not only a perfectly definite statement of the principles upon which they would be willing to conclude peace, but also an equally definite program of the concrete application of those principles. The representatives of the Central Powers, on their part, presented an outline of settlement which, if much less definite, seemed susceptible of liberal interpretation until their specific program of practical terms was added. That program proposed no concessions at all, either to the sovereignty of Russia or to the preferences of the population with whose fortunes it dealt, but meant, in a word, that the Central Empires were to keep every foot of territory their armed forces had occupied--every province, every city, every point of vantage--as a permanent addition to their territories and their power. It is a reasonable conjecture that the general principles of settlement which they at first suggested originated with the more liberal statesmen of Germany and Austria, the men who have begun to feel the force of their own people's thought and purpose, while the concrete terms of actual settlement came from the military leaders who have no thought but to keep what they have got. The negotiations have been broken off. The Russian representatives were sincere and in earnest. They cannot entertain such proposals of conquest and domination.

SIGNIFICANCE IN PARLEYS

The whole incident is full of significance. It is also full of perplexity. With whom are 152the Russian representatives dealing? For whom are the representatives of the Central Empires speaking? Are they speaking for the majorities of their respective parliaments, or for the minority parties--that military and imperialistic minority which has so far dominated their whole policy and controlled the affairs of Turkey and the Balkan states, which have felt obliged to become their associates in this war? The Russian representatives have insisted, very justly, very wisely, and in the true spirit of modern democracy, that the conferences they have been holding with the Teutonic and Turkish statesmen should be held within open, not closed, doors, and all the world has been audience, as was desired.

To whom have we been listening, then? To those who speak the spirit and intention of the resolution of the German Reichstag of the 9th of July last, the spirit and intention of the Liberal leaders and parties of Germany, or to those who resist and defy that spirit and intention and insist upon conquest and subjugation? Or are we listening, in fact, to both, unreconciled and in open and hopeless contradiction? These are very serious and pregnant questions. Upon the answer to them depends the peace of the world.

But, whatever the results of the parleys at Brest-Litovsk, whatever the confusions of counsel and of purpose in the utterances of the 153spokesmen of the Central Empires, they have again attempted to acquaint the world with their objects in the war and have again challenged their adversaries to say what their objects are and what sort of settlement they would deem just and satisfactory. There is no good reason why that challenge should not be responded to and responded to with the utmost candor. We did not wait for it. Not once, but again and again, we have laid our whole thought and purpose before the world, not in general terms only, but each time with sufficient definition to make it clear what sort of definitive terms of settlement must necessarily spring out of them.

LLOYD GEORGE'S AIMS APPROVED

Within the last week Mr. Lloyd George has spoken with admirable candor and in admirable spirit for the people and Government of Great Britain. There is no confusion of counsel among the adversaries of the Central Powers, no uncertainty of principle, no vagueness of detail. The only secrecy of counsel, the only lack of fearless frankness, the only failure to make definite statement of the objects of the war lies with Germany and her allies. The issues of life and death hang upon these definitions. No statesman who has the least conception of his responsibility ought for a moment to permit himself to continue this 154tragical and appalling outpouring of blood and treasure unless he is sure beyond a peradventure that the objects of the vital sacrifice are part and parcel of the very life of society, and that the people for whom he speaks think them right and imperative, as he does.

There is, moreover, a voice calling for these definitions of principle and of purpose which is, it seems to me, more thrilling and more compelling than any of the many moving voices with which the troubled air of the world is filled. It is the voice of the Russian people. They are prostrate and all but helpless, it would seem, before the grim power of Germany, which has hitherto known no relenting and no pity. Their power apparently is shattered. And yet their soul is not subservient. They will not yield either in principle or in action. Their conception of what is right, of what it is humane and honorable for them to accept, has been stated with a frankness, a largeness of view, a generosity of spirit and a universal human sympathy which must challenge the admiration of every friend of mankind; and they have refused to compound their ideals or desert others that they themselves may be safe.

WOULD LIKE TO AID RUSSIA

They call to us to say what it is that we desire--in what, if in anything, our purpose and our spirit differ from theirs; and I believe 155that the people of the United States would wish me to respond with utter simplicity and frankness. Whether their present leaders believe it or not, it is our heartfelt desire and hope that some way may be opened whereby we may be privileged to assist the people of Russia to attain their utmost hope of liberty and ordered peace.

It will be our wish and purpose that the processes of peace, when they are begun, shall be absolutely open, and that they shall involve and permit henceforth no secret understandings of any kind. The day of conquest and aggrandizement is gone by; so is also the day of secret covenants entered into in the interest of particular governments and likely, at some unlooked-for moment, to upset the peace of the world. It is this happy fact, now clear to the view of every public man whose thoughts do not still linger in an age that is dead and gone, which makes it possible for every nation whose purposes are consistent with justice and the peace of the world to avow now, or at any other time, the objects it has in view.

We entered this war because violations of right had occurred which touched us to the quick and made the life of our own people impossible unless they were corrected and the world secured once for all against their recurrence. What we demand in this war, therefore, 156is nothing peculiar to ourselves. It is that the world be made fit and safe to live in; and particularly that it be made safe for every peace-loving nation which, like our own, wishes to live its own life, determine its own institutions, be assured of justice and fair dealing by the other peoples of the world as against force and selfish aggression. All the peoples of the world are in effect partners in this interest, and for our own part we see very clearly that unless justice be done to others it will not be done to us.

THE DEFINITE PROGRAM

The program of the world's peace, therefore, is our program, and that program, the only possible program, as we see it, is this:

I. Open covenants of peace, openly arrived at, after which there shall be no private international understandings of any kind, but diplomacy shall proceed always frankly and in the public view.

II. Absolute freedom of navigation upon the seas, outside territorial waters, alike in peace and in war, except as the seas may be closed in whole or in part by international action for the enforcement of international covenants.

III. The removal, so far as possible, of all economic barriers and the establishment of an equality of trade conditions among all the nations 157consenting to the peace and associating themselves for its maintenance.

IV. Adequate guarantees given and taken that national armaments will be reduced to the lowest point consistent with domestic safety.

V. A free, open-minded and absolutely impartial adjustment of all colonial claims, based upon a strict observance of the principle that in determining all such questions of sovereignty the interests of the populations concerned must have equal weight with the equitable claims of the Government whose title is to be determined.

VI. The evacuation of all Russian territory and such a settlement of all questions affecting Russia as will secure the best and freest co-operation of the other nations of the world in obtaining for her an unhampered and unembarrassed opportunity for the independent determination of her own political development and national policy and assure her of a sincere welcome into the society of free nations under institutions of her own choosing; and, more than a welcome, assistance also of every kind that she may need and may herself desire. The treatment accorded Russia by her sister nations will be the acid test of their good will, of their comprehension of her needs as distinguished from their own interests and of their intelligent and unselfish sympathy.

BELGIUM MUST BE RESTORED

VII. Belgium, the whole world will agree, must be evacuated and restored, without any attempt to limit the sovereignty which she enjoys in common with all other free nations. No other single act will serve as this will serve to restore confidence among the nations in the laws which they have themselves set and determined for the government of their relations with one another. Without this healing act the whole structure and validity of international law is forever impaired.

VIII. All French territory should be freed and the invaded portions restored, and the wrong done to France by Prussia in 1871 in the matter of Alsace-Lorraine, which has unsettled the peace of the world for nearly fifty years, should be righted, in order that peace may once more be made secure in the interest of all.

IX. A readjustment of the frontiers of Italy should be effected along clearly recognizable lines of nationality.

X. The peoples of Austria-Hungary, whose place among the nations we wish to see safeguarded and assured, should be accorded the freest opportunity of autonomous development.

XI. Rumania, Serbia, and Montenegro should be evacuated; occupied territories restored; Serbia accorded free and secure access to the sea; and the relations of the several Balkan states to one another determined by friendly counsel along historically established lines of allegiance and nationality; and international guarantees of the political and economic independence and territorial integrity of the several Balkan states should be entered into.

XII. The Turkish portions of the present Ottoman Empire should be assured a secure sovereignty, but the other nationalities which are now under Turkish rule should be assured an undoubted security of life and an absolutely unmolested opportunity of autonomous development, and the Dardanelles should be permanently opened as a free passage to the ships and commerce of all nations under international guarantees.

INDEPENDENCE FOR POLAND

XIII. An independent Polish state should be erected which should include the territories inhabited by indisputably Polish populations, which should be assured a free and secure access 159to the sea, and whose political and economic independence and territorial integrity should be guaranteed by international covenant.

XIV. A general association of nations must be formed under specific covenants for the purpose of affording mutual guarantees of political independence and territorial integrity to great and small states alike.

160

In regard to these essential rectifications of wrong and assertions of right, we feel ourselves to be intimate partners of all the Governments and peoples associated together against the imperialists. We cannot be separated in interest or divided in purpose. We stand together until the end.

For such arrangements and covenants we are willing to fight, and to continue to fight, until they are achieved; but only because we wish the right to prevail and desire a just and stable peace, such as can be secured only by removing the chief provocations to war, which this program does remove. We have no jealousy of German greatness, and there is nothing in this program that impairs it. We grudge her no achievement or distinction of learning or of pacific enterprise, such as have made her record very bright and very enviable. We do not wish to injure her or to block in any way her legitimate influence or power. We do not wish to fight her either with arms or with hostile arrangements of trade, if she is willing to associate herself with us and the other peace-loving nations of the world in covenants of justice and law and fair dealing. We wish her only to accept a place of equality among the peoples of the world--the new world in which we now live--instead of a place of mastery.

161

GERMANY'S SPOKESMEN AN ISSUE

Neither do we presume to suggest to her any alteration or modification of her institutions. But it is necessary, we must frankly say, and necessary as a preliminary to any intelligent dealings with her on our part, that we should know whom her spokesmen speak for when they speak to us, whether for the Reichstag majority or for the military party and the men whose creed is imperial domination.

We have spoken now surely in terms too concrete to admit of any further doubt or question. An evident principle runs through the whole program I have outlined. It is the principle of justice to all peoples and nationalities and their right to live on equal terms of liberty and safety with one another, whether they be strong or weak. Unless this principle be made its foundation, no part of the structure of international justice can stand. The people of the United States could act upon no other principle, and to the vindication of this principle they are ready to devote their lives, their honor and everything that they possess. The moral climax of this, the culminating and final war for human liberty, has come, and they are ready to put their own strength, their own highest purpose, their own integrity and devotion to the test.

163

APPENDIX

STATE DEPARTMENT'S REVISED LIST OF NATIONS AT WAR WHICH HAVE BROKEN RELATIONS

DECLARATIONS OF WAR

The country declaring war is named first.

Austria--Belgium, Aug. 28, 1914.
Austria--Japan, Aug. 27, 1914.
Austria--Montenegro, Aug. 9, 1914.
Austria--Russia, Aug. 6, 1914.
Austria--Serbia, July 28, 1914.
Brazil--Germany, Oct. 26, 1917.
Bulgaria--Serbia, Oct. 14, 1915.
China--Austria, Aug. 14, 1917.
China--Germany, Aug. 14, 1917.
Cuba--Germany, April 7, 1917.
France--Austria, Aug. 13, 1914.
France--Bulgaria, Oct. 16, 1915.
France--Germany, Aug. 3, 1914.
France--Turkey, Nov. 5, 1914.
Germany--Belgium, Aug. 4, 1914.
Germany--France, Aug. 3, 1914.
Germany--Portugal, March 9, 1916.
Germany--Rumania, Sept. 14, 1916.
Germany--Russia, Aug. 1, 1914.
Great Britain--Austria, Aug. 13, 1914.
164 Great Britain--Bulgaria, Oct. 15, 1915.
Great Britain--Germany, Aug. 4, 1914.
Great Britain--Turkey, Nov. 5, 1914.
Greece--Bulgaria, Nov. 28, 1916. (Provisional Government.)
Greece--Bulgaria, July 2, 1917. (Government of Alexander.)
Greece--Germany, Nov. 28, 1916. (Provisional Government.)
Greece--Germany, July 2, 1917. (Government of Alexander.)

Italy--Austria, May 24, 1915.
Italy--Bulgaria, Oct. 19, 1915.
Italy--Germany, Aug. 28, 1916.
Italy--Turkey, Aug. 21, 1915.
Japan--Germany, Aug. 28, 1914.
Liberia--Germany, Aug. 4, 1917.
Montenegro--Austria, Aug. 8, 1914.
Montenegro--Germany, Aug. 9, 1914.
Panama--Germany, April 7, 1917.
Panama--Austria, Dec. 10, 1917.
Portugal--Germany, Nov. 23, 1914. (Resolutions passed authorizing military intervention as ally of England.)
Portugal--Germany, May 19, 1915. (Military aid granted.)
Rumania--Austria, Aug. 27, 1916. (Allies of Austria also consider it a declaration.)
Russia--Bulgaria, Oct. 19, 1915.
Russia--Turkey, Nov. 3, 1914.
San Marino--Austria, May 24, 1915.
Serbia--Bulgaria, Oct. 16, 1915.
Serbia--Germany, Aug. 6, 1914.
Serbia--Turkey, Dec. 2, 1914.
Siam--Austria, July 22, 1917.
Siam--Germany, July 22, 1917.
Turkey--Allies, Nov. 23, 1914.
Turkey--Rumania, Aug. 29, 1916.
165 United States--Austria-Hungary, Dec. 7, 1917.
United States--Germany, April 6, 1917.

SEVERANCE OF DIPLOMATIC RELATIONS

Austria--Japan, Aug. 26, 1914.
Austria--Portugal, March 16, 1916.
Austria--Serbia, July 26, 1914.
Austria--United States, April 8, 1917.

Bolivia--Germany, April 14, 1917.
Brazil--Germany, April 11,1917.
China--Germany, March 14, 1917.
Costa Rica--Germany, Sept. 21, 1917.
Ecuador--Germany, Dec. 7, 1917.
Egypt--Germany, Aug. 13, 1914.
France--Austria, Aug. 10, 1914.
Greece--Turkey, July 2, 1917. (Government of Alexander.)
Greece--Austria, July 2, 1917. (Government of Alexander.)
Guatemala--Germany, April 27, 1917.
Haiti--Germany, June 17, 1917.
Honduras--Germany, May 17, 1917.
Nicaragua--Germany, May 18, 1917.
Peru--Germany, Oct. 6, 1917.
Turkey--United States, April 20, 1917.
United States--Germany, Feb. 3, 1917.
Uruguay--Germany, Oct. 7, 1917.

--From the Official Bulletin of the Committee on Public Information.

POPULATION OF THE NATIONS

Austria (including Hungary)	50,000,000
Belgium	7,571,387
Bolivia	2,520,538
Brazil	22,992,937
Bulgaria	4,755,000
China	413,000,000
Costa Rica	427,604
Cuba	2,406,117
Ecuador	1,500,000
Egypt	12,170,000
France	39,601,509

Germany	66,715,000
Great Britain	40,834,790
Greece	5,000,000
Guatemala	2,092,824
Haiti	2,030,000
Honduras	592,675
Italy	35,598,000
Japan	53,696,358
Liberia	2,060,000
Montenegro	520,000
Nicaragua	689,891
Panama	386,891
Peru	4,500,000
Portugal	5,857,895
Rumania	7,600,000
Russia	175,137,000
San Marino	10,655
Serbia	4,600,000
Siam	6,000,000
Turkey	21,274,000
United States	102,826,309
Uruguay	1,255,914

THE END